THE CHARLES G. FINNEY
MEMORIAL LIBRARY

Evangelistic Sermon Series
- So Great Salvation
- The Guilt of Sin
- True and False Repentance
- God's Love for a Sinning World

Revival Sermon Series
- Victory Over the World
- True Saints
- True Submission

Sermons on Prayer
- Prevailing Prayer

TRUE

SAINTS

TRUE SAINTS

Revival Messages

CHARLES G. FINNEY

KREGEL PUBLICATIONS
GRAND RAPIDS, MICHIGAN 49501

Library of Congress Catalog Card Number 66-24880
ISBN 0-8254-2622-7

This series of sermons selected from
LECTURES TO PROFESSING CHRISTIANS
by Charles G. Finney

First Printing 1975
Second Printing 1978

080618

Printed in the United States of America

PUBLISHER'S FOREWORD

Why this new edition of the sermons of Charles Grandison Finney? Because in many ways the days in which we are living are a duplicate of the day and situation in which Finney himself proclaimed the message which God had given him — the call to evangelism and to revival. These messages speak to our day in no uncertain sound for conditions within the church, and in the world around, call for a voice from God, a resounding clarion call for return to the Biblical standard of Christian life, and the God-ordained plan of redemption and revival.

These have been chosen and arranged with the needs of the world and church today in view. They are as applicable in this day of falling away and departure from the faith as they were in Finney's day. Heart-searching and uncompromising, they cut away the froth and frills so apparent in much modern preaching to reveal God's message for a sinning world, a world seemingly intent upon self-destruction and self-aggrandizement.

It is the publisher's prayer that these messages in their new form will convey God's message to our needy world, revealing His will and purpose for His Church — and His divine plan of salvation for an unbelieving generation.

The Publishers

CONTENTS

1

SELF DECEIVERS

"But be ye doers of the word, and not hearers only, deceiving your own selves." James 1:22.

THERE are two extremes in religion, equally false and equally fatal. And there are two classes of hypocrites that occupy these two extremes. The first class make religion to consist altogether in the belief of certain abstract doctrines, or what they call faith, and lay little or no stress on good works. The other class make religion to consist altogether in good works, (I mean, dead works) and lay little or no stress on faith in Jesus Christ, but hope for salvation by their own deeds. The Jews belonged generally to the last-mentioned class. Their religious teachers taught them that they would be saved by obedience to the ceremonial law. And therefore, when Paul began to preach, he seems to have attacked more especially this error of the Jews. He was determined to carry the main question, that men are justified by faith in Jesus Christ, in opposition to the doctrine of the scribes and pharisees, that salvation is by obedience to the law. And he pressed this point so earnestly, in his preaching and in his epistles, that he carried it, and settled the faith of the church in the great doctrine of justification by faith. And then certain individuals in the church laid hold of this doctrine and carried it to the opposite extreme, and maintained that men are saved by faith altogether, irrespective of works of any kind. They overlooked the plain principle, that genuine faith always results in good works, and is itself a good work.

I said that these two extremes, that which makes religion to consist altogether in outward works and that which makes it consist altogether in faith, are equally false and equally fatal. Those who make religion consist altogether in good works, overlook the fact that works themselves are not acceptable to God unless they proceed from faith. For without faith it is impossible to please him. And those who make religion consist altogether in faith, overlook the fact that true faith always works by love, and invariably produces the works of love.

They are equally fatal, because, on the one hand, without faith persons cannot be pardoned or justified; and on the other, without sanctification they cannot be fitted either for the employments or enjoyments of heaven. Let a sinner turn from his sins altogether, and suppose his works to be as perfect as he thinks them to be, and yet he could not be pardoned without faith in the atonement of Jesus Christ. And so if any one supposed that he could be justified by faith while his works were evil, he ought to know that without sanctification his faith is but dead, and cannot even be the instrument of his justification.

It appears that the apostle James, in this epistle, designed to put this matter upon the right ground, and show exactly where the truth lay, and to explain the necessity, and reason of the necessity, of both faith and good works. This epistle is a very practical one, and it meets full in the face all the great practical questions of the day, and decides them.

Doctrines in religion are of two classes, those which refer to God, and those which refer to human practice. Many confine their idea of religious doctrines to the former class. They think nothing is properly called doctrine but what respects God, his attributes, mode of existence, decrees, and so on. When I gave notice that I should commence a course of "Practical Lectures," I hope you did not understand me to mean that the lectures would not be doctrinal, or would have no doctrine in them. My design is to preach, if the Lord will, a course of lectures on practical doctrines. The doctrine which I propose to consider now, is this—That professor of religion who does not practice what he admits to be true, is self-deceived.

There are two classes of hypocrites among professors of religion, those that deceive others and those that deceive themselves. One class of hypocrites are those that, under a specious outside of morality and religion, cover up the enmity of their hearts against God, and lead others to think they are very pious people. Thus the pharisees obtained the reputation of being remarkably pious, by their outside show of religion, their alms and their long prayers. The other class is that referred to in the text, who do not deceive others but themselves. These are orthodox in sentiment, but loose in practice. They seem to suppose religion to consist in a parcel of notions, without regard to practice, and thus deceive themselves by thinking they are good Christians while destitute of true holiness. They are hearers of the word but not doers. They love orthodox preaching, and take great pleasure in hearing the abstract doctrines of religion exhibited, and perhaps have flights of imagination and glowing feelings in view of the character and government of God, but they are not careful to practise the precepts of God's word, nor are they pleased with the preaching of those doctrines which relate to human practice.

Perhaps there are some present to-night of both these classes of hypocrites. Now mark! I am not going to preach to-night to those of you who, by great strictness of

morals and outside show of religion, deceive others. I ad-
dress, now, those of you who do not practise what you
know to be true—who are hearers and not doers. Perhaps
I had better say, to secure attention, that it is very proba-
ble there are a number here now of this character. I do
not know your names; but I wish you to understand, that
if you are that character, you are the persons I am speaking to, just as if I called out your names. I mean you.
You hear the word, and believe it in theory, while you
deny it in practice. I say to you, that " you deceive yourselves." The text proves it. Here you have an express
" Thus saith the Lord " for it, that all such characters are
self-deceivers. I might quote a number of other passages
of scripture, that are to the point, and there leave it. But
I wish to call your attention to some other considerations
beside the direct scripture testimony.

In the first place, you do not *truly* believe the word.
You hear it, and admit it to be true, but you do not truly
believe it. And here let me say, that persons are themselves liable to deception on this point. Not that their
consciousness deceives them, but they do not understand
what it is that consciousness testifies. Two things are indispensable to evangelical, or saving faith. The first is,
intellectual conviction of the truth of a thing. And here
I do not mean merely the abstract truth of it, but in its
bearing on you. The truth, in its relation to you, or its
bearing on your conduct, must be received intellectually.
And then true faith includes a corresponding state of the
heart. This always enters into the essence of true faith.
When a man's understanding is convinced, and he admits
the truth in its relation to himself, then there must be a
hearty approbation of it in its bearing or relation to himself. Both these states of mind are indispensable to true
faith. Intellectual conviction of the truth is not saving
faith. But intellectual conviction, when accompanied with

a corresponding state of the affections, is saving faith. Hence it follows that where there is true saving faith, there is always corresponding conduct. The conduct always follows the real faith. Just as certain as the will controls the conduct, men will act as they believe. Suppose I say to a man, Do you believe this? "Yes, I believe it." What does he mean ? A mere intellectual conviction ? He may have that, and yet not have faith.

A man may even feel an approbation of an abstract truth. This is what many persons suppose to be faith—the approbation which they feel for the character and government of God, and for the plan of salvation, when viewed abstractedly. Many persons, when they hear an eloquent sermon on the attributes or government of God, are set all in a glow at the excellency displayed, when they have not a particle of true faith. I have heard of an infidel, who would be moved even to ecstacy at such themes. The rational mind is so constituted that it naturally and necessarily approves of truth when viewed abstractedly. The wickedest devils in hell love it, if they can see it without its relation to themselves. If they could see the gospel without any relation that interferes with their own selfishness, they would not only see it to be true, but would heartily approve of it. All hell, if they could view God in his absolute existence, without any relation to themselves, would heartily approve his character. The reason why wicked men and devils hate God is, because they see him in relation to themselves. Their hearts rise up in rebellion, because they see him opposed to their selfishness.

Here is the source of a grand delusion among men in regard to religion. They see it to be true, and they really rejoice in contemplating it ; they do not enter into its relation to themselves, and so they love to hear such preaching, and say they are fed by it. But mark ! They go away and do not practise. See that man ! he is sick, and his feelings are tender. In view of Christ, as a kind and tender Saviour, his heart melts and he feels strong emotions of approbation towards Jesus Christ. Why? For the very same reasons that he would feel strong emotions toward the hero of a romance. But he does not obey Christ. He never practises one thing out of obedience to Christ, but views him abstractedly, and is delighted with his glorious and lovely character, while he himself remains in the gall of bitterness. Thus it is apparent that your faith must be an efficient faith, such as regulates your practice and produces good works, or it is not the faith of the gospel, it is no real faith at all.

Again. It is further manifest that you are deceiving yourselves, because all true religion consists in obedience. And therefore, however much you may approve of Christianity, you have no religion unless you obey it. In saying that all religion consists in obedience, I do not mean OUTWARD obedience. But faith itself, true faith, works by love, and produces corresponding action. There is no real obedience but the obedience of the heart; love is the fulfilling of the law; and religion consists in the obedience of the heart, with a corresponding course of life. The man, therefore, who hears the truth, and approves it, and does not practise it, deceiveth himself. He is like the man beholding his natural face in a glass; for he beholdeth himself, and goeth his way, and straightway forgetteth what manner of a man he was.

Again. That state of mind which you mistake for religion, an intellectual conviction of truth, and approval of it in the abstract, so far from being evidence that you are pious, is as common to the wicked as to the good, whenever they can be brought to look at it abstractedly. This is the reason why it is often so difficult to convince sinners that they are opposed to God and his truth. Men are so constituted that they do approve of virtue, and do admire the character and government of God, and would approve and admire every truth in the Bible, if they could view it abstractedly, and without any relation to themselves. And when they sit under preaching that holds up the truth in such a way, that it has not much of a practical bearing on themselves, they may sit for years and never consider that they are opposed to God and his government.

And I am more and more persuaded, that great multitudes are to be found in all our congregations, where the abstract doctrines of the gospel are much preached, who like the preaching and like to hear about God, and all these things, and yet are unconverted. And no doubt multitudes of them get into the churches, because they love orthodox preaching, when, after all, it is manifest that they are not doers of the word. And here is the difficulty; they have not had that searching preaching that made them see the truth in its bearing on themselves. And now they are in the church, whenever the truth is preached in its practical relation to them, they show the enmity of their hearts unchanged, by rising up in opposition to truth.

They took it for granted that they were Christians, and so joined the church, because they could hear sound doctrinal preaching and approve of it, or because they read the Bible and approved of it. If their faith be not so practical as to influence their conduct, if they do not view the truth in its relation to their own practice, their faith does not affect them so much as the FAITH OF THE DEVIL.

CONCLUSION

1. Great injury has been done by false representations regarding the wickedness of real Christians.

A celebrated preacher, not long since, is said to have given this definition of a Christian—"A little grace and a great deal of devil." I utterly deny this definition. It is

false and ruinous. A great deal is said that makes an im
pression that real Christians are the wickedest beings on
the face of the earth. It is true that when they do sin
they incur great guilt. For a Christian to sin is highly
criminal. And it is also true that enlightened Christians
see in their sins great wickedness. When they compare
their obligations with their lives, they are greatly humbled,
and express their humility in very strong language. But
it is not true that they are as bad as the devil, or anywhere
in the neighborhood of it. This is perfectly demonstrable.
When they do sin, their sins have great aggravation, and
appear extremely wicked in the sight of God. But to suppose that men are real Christians while they live in the
service of the devil, and have little of even the appearance
of religion, is a sentiment that is not only false but of very
dangerous tendency. It is calculated to encourage all
that class of hypocrites who are Antinomians, and to encourage backsliders, as well as to do a great injury to the
cause of Christ in the estimation of scorners. The truth
is, those who do not obey God are not Christians. The
contrary doctrine is ruinous to the churches, by filling
them up with multitudes whose claim to piety depends on
their adoption of certain notions, while they never heartily
intended to obey the requirements of the gospel in their
lives.

2. Those who are so much more zealous for doctrines
than for practice, and who lay much more stress on that
class of doctrines which relate to God than on that class
which relate to their own conduct, are Antinomians.

There are many who will receive that class of the doctrines of the Bible that relate to God and approve and love
them, who have not a particle of religion. Those who are
never "fed," as they call it, on any preaching but that of
certain abstract points of doctrine, are Antinomians. They
are the very persons against whom the apostle James wrote

this epistle. They make religion to consist in a set of notions, while they do not lead holy lives.

3. That class of professors of religion who never like to hear about God or his attributes, or mode of existence, the Trinity, decrees, election, and the like, but lay all stress on religious practice to the exclusion of religious doctrine, are pharisees.

They make great pretensions to outward piety, and perhaps to inward flights of emotion of a certain poetical cast, while they will not receive the great truths that relate to God, but deny the fundamental doctrines of the gospel.

4. The proper end and tendency of all right doctrine, when truly believed, is to produce correct practice.

Wherever you find a man's practice heretical, you may oe sure his belief is heretical too. The faith that he holds in his heart is just as heretical as his life. He may not be heretical in his notions and theories. He may be right there, even on the very points where he is heretical in practice. But he does not really believe it.

For illustration : See that careless sinner there, grasping wealth, and rushing headlong in the search for riches. Does that man truly believe he is ever going to die ? Perhaps you will say, he knows he must die. But I say, while he is in this attitude, he does not actually believe he is ever going to die. The subject is one which is not before his thoughts at all. And thus it is, therefore, impossible that he should believe it in his utter thoughtlessness. You ask him if he expect ever to die, and he will reply, "O yes, I know I must die ; all men are mortal." As soon as he turns his thoughts to it, he assents to the truth. And if you could fasten the conviction on his mind till he is really and permanently impressed with it, he would-infallibly change his conduct, and live for another world instead of this. It is just so in religion ; whatever a man really believes is just as certain to control his practice as that the will governs the conduct.

5. The church has for a long time acted too much on the Antinomial policy.

She has been sticklish for the more abstract doctrines, and left the more practical too much out of view. She has laid greater stress on orthodoxy in those doctrines that are not practical, than in those that are practical. Look at the creeds of the church, and see how they all lay the main stress on those doctrines that have little relation to our practice. A man may be the greatest heretic on points of practice, provided he is not openly profane and vicious, and yet maintain a good standing in the church, whether his life corresponds with the gospel or not. Is not this monstrous ? And hence we see that when it is attempted to purify the church in regard to practical errors, she cannot bear it. Why else is it that so much excitement is produced by attempting to clear the church from participation in sins of intemperance, and Sabbath-breaking, and slavery ? Why is it so difficult to induce the church to do anything effectual for the conversion of the world ? Oh, when shall the church be purified, or the world converted? Not till it is a settled point, that heresy in practice is the proof of heresy in belief. Not while a man may deny the whole gospel in his practice every day, and yet maintain his standing in the church as a good Christian.

6. See how a minister may be deceived in regard to the state of his congregation.

He preaches a good deal on the abstract doctrines, that do not immediately relate to practice, and his people say they are fed, and rejoice in it, and he thinks they are growing in grace, when in fact it is no certain sign that there is any religion among them. It is manifest that this is not certain evidence. But if when he preaches practical doctrines, his people show that they love the truth in relation to themselves, and show it by practising it, then they give evidence of real love to the truth.

If a minister find that his people love abstract doctrinal preaching, but that when he comes to press the practical doctrines they rebel, he may be sure that if they have any religion, it is in a low state ; and if he find, on fair trial, that he cannot bring them up to it, so as to receive practical doctrine, he may be satisfied they have not a particle of religion, but are a mere company of Antinomians, who think they can go to heaven on a dead faith in abstract orthodoxy.

7. See what a vast multitude of professors of religion there are who are deceiving themselves.

Many suppose they are Christians from the emotions they feel in view of the truth, when in fact what they receive is truth presented to their minds in such a way that they do not see its bearing on themselves. If you bring the truth so to bear on them, as to destroy their pride and cut them off from their worldliness, such professors resist it. Look abroad upon the church. See what a multitude of orthodox churches and orthodox Christians live and feed upon the abstract doctrines of religion from year to year. Then look farther at their lives, and see how little influence their professed belief has upon their practice. Have they saving faith ? It cannot be. I do not mean to say that none of these church members are pious, but I de say that those who do not adopt in practice what they admit in theory—who are hearers of the word but not doers, deceive themselves.

Inquire now how many of you really believe the truths you hear preached. I have proposed to preach a course of "practical" lectures. I do not mean that I shall preach lectures that have no doctrine in them. That is not preaching at all. But what I desire is, to see whether you will, as a church, do what you believe to be true. If

I do not succeed in convincing you that any doctrine I
may maintain is really true, that is another affair. That
is reason enough why you should not do it. But if I do
succeed in proving from the scriptures, and convincing
your understanding, that it is true, and yet you do not
practice it, I shall then have the evidence before my own
eyes what your character is, and no longer deceive myself
with the idea that this is a Christian church.

Are you conscious that the gospel is producing a practical effect upon you, according to your advancement in
knowledge ? Is it weaning you from the world ? Do you
find this to be your experience, that when you receive any
practical truth into your minds you love it, and love to
feel its application to yourself, and take pleasure in practising it ? If you are not growing in grace, becoming
more and more holy, yielding yourselves up to the influence of the gospel, you are deceiving yourselves. How is
it now with you who are elders of this church ? How is
it with you who are heads of families—all of you ? When
you hear a sermon, do you seize hold of it and take it
home to you, and practise it ? Or do you receive it into
your minds, and approve of it, and never practise it ?
Woe to that man who admits the truth, and yet turns
away and does not practise it, like the man beholding his
natural face in a glass turning away and forgetting what
manner of man he was.

2

FALSE PROFESSORS

"They feared the Lord, and served their own gods." 2 Kings 17:33.

WHEN the ten tribes of Israel were carried away captive by the king of Assyria, their places were supplied with strangers of different idolatrous nations, who knew nothing of the religion of the Jews. Very soon the wild beasts increased in the country, and the lions destroyed multitudes of the people, and they thought it was because they did not know the god of the country, and had therefore ignorantly transgressed his religion, and offended him, and he had sent the lions among them as a punishment. So they applied to the king, who told them to get one of the priests of the Israelites to teach them the manner of the god of the land. They took this advice, and obtained one of the priests to come to Bethel and teach them the religious ceremonies and modes of worship that had been practised there. And he taught them to fear Jehovah, as the God of that country. But still they did not receive him as the only God. They feared him ; that is, they feared his anger and his judgments, and to avert these, they performed the prescribed rites. But they "served" their own gods. They kept up their idolatrous worship, and this was what they loved and preferred, though they felt obliged to pay some reverence to Jehovah, as the God of that country. There are still multitudes of persons, professing to fear God, and perhaps possessing a certain kind of the fear of the Lord, who, nevertheless, serve their own gods—they have other things to which their hearts are supremely devoted, and other objects in which they mainly put their trust.

There are, as you know, two kinds of fear. There is that fear of the Lord which is the beginning of wisdom, which is founded in love. There is also a slavish fear, which is a mere dread of evil, and is purely selfish. This is the kind of fear which is possessed by those people spoken of in the text. They were afraid Jehovah would send his judgments upon them, if they did not perform certain rites and this was the motive they had for paying him worship. Those who have this fear are supremely selfish, and while they profess to reverence Jehovah, have other gods whom they love and serve.

There are several classes of persons to whom this is applicable, and my object to-night is to describe some of them, in such a way, that those of you here, who possess this character, may know yourselves, and may see how it is that your neighbors know you and understand your rea. characters.

To serve a person is to be obedient to the will and devoted to the interests of that individual. It is not properly called serving where only certain acts are performed, without entering into the service of the person ; but to serve, is to make it a business to do the will and promote the interest of the person. To serve God is to make religion the main business of life. It is to devote one's self, heart, life, powers, time, influence, and all, to promote the interests of God, to build up the kingdom of God, and to advance the glory of God. Who are they who, while they profess to fear the Lord, serve their own gods ?

I answer, first, all those of you who have not heartily and practically renounced the ownership of your possessions, and given them up to God.

It is self-evident that if you have not done this, you are not serving God. Suppose a gentleman were to employ a clerk to take care of his store, and suppose the clerk were to continue to attend to his own business, and when asked to do what is necessary for his employer, who pays him his wages, he should reply, "I really have so much business of my own to attend to, that I have no time to do these things;" would not everybody cry out against such a servant, and say he was not serving his employer at all, his time is not his own, it is paid for, and he but served himself? So where a man has not renounced the ownership of himself, not only in thought, but practically, he has not taken the first lesson in religion. He is not serving the Lord, but serving his own gods.

2. That man who does not make the business in which he is engaged a part of his religion, does not serve God.

You hear a man say, sometimes, I am so much engaged all day in the world, or in worldly business, that I have not time to serve God. He thinks he serves God a little while in the morning, and then attends to his worldly business. That man, you may rely on it, left his religion where he said his prayers. He is willing, perhaps, to give God the time before breakfast, before he gets ready to go to his own business; but as soon as that is over, away he goes to his own work. He fears the Lord enough, perhaps, to go through his prayers night and morning, but he serves his own gods. That man's religion is the laughing stock of hell! He prays very devoutly, and then, instead of engaging in his business for God, he is serving himself. No doubt the idols are well satisfied with the arrangement, but God is wholly displeased.

3. But again: Those of you are serving your own gods, who devote to Jehovah that which costs you little or nothing.

There are many who make religion consist in certain acts of piety that do not interefere with their selfishness. You pray in the morning in your family, because you can do it then very conveniently, but do not suffer the service of Jehovah to interfere with the service of your gods, or to stand in the way of your getting rich, or enjoying the world. The gods you serve make no complaint of being slighted or neglected for the service of Jehovah.

4. All that class are serving their own gods, who suppose that the six days of the week belong to themselves, and that the Sabbath only is God's day.

There are multitudes who suppose that the week is man's time, and the Sabbath only God's, and that they have a right to do their own work during the week, and to serve themselves, and promote their own interests, if they will only keep the Sabbath strictly, and serve God on the Sabbath. For instance : a celebrated preacher, in illustrating the wickedness of breaking the Sabbath, used this illustration—" Suppose a man, having seven dollars in his pocket, should meet a beggar in great distress, and give him six dollars, keeping only one for himself ; and the beggar, seeing that he retained one dollar, should return and rob him of that ; would not every heart despise his baseness?" You see it embodies this idea—that it is very ungrateful to break the Sabbath since God has given to men six days for their own, to serve themselves, and only reserved the Sabbath to himself, and to rob God of the seventh day is base ingratitude.

You that do this do not serve God at all. If you are selfish during the week, you are selfish altogether. To suppose you had any real piety would imply that you were converted every Sabbath and unconverted every Monday. If a man would serve himself all the week and really possess religion on the Sabbath, he requires to be converted for it. But is this the idea of the Sabbath, that it is a day to serve God in exclusive of other days ? Is God in need of your services on the Sabbath to keep his work on ? God requires all your services as much on the six days as on the Sabbath, only he has appropriated the Sabbath to peculiar duties, and required its observance as a day of rest from bodily toil and from those fatiguing cares and labors that concern the present world. But because God uses means in accomplishing his purposes, and men have bodies as well as souls, and the gospel is to be spread and sustained by the things of this world, therefore God requires you to work all the six days at your secular employments. But it is all for his service, as much as the worship of the Sabbath. The Sabbath is no more given for the service of God than Monday. You have no more right to serve yourselves on Monday than you have on the Sabbath. If any of you have thus considered the matter, and imagined that the six days of the week were your own time, it shows that you are supremely selfish. I beg of you not to consider that in prayer and on the Sabbath you are serving God at all, if the rest of the time you are considered as serving yourself. You have never known the radical principle of serving the Lord.

5. Those are serving themselves, or their own gods, who will not make any sacrifices of personal ease and comfort in religion.

For instance, there are multitudes who object to free churches on this ground, that they require a sacrifice of personal gratification. They talk like this : " We wish to sit with our families ; " or, " We want our seats cushioned," or " We always like to sit in the same place." They admit that free churches are necessary, in order to make the gospel accessible to the thousands that are going to hell in this city. But they cannot make these little sacrifices, to throw open the doors of God's house to this mass of impenitent sinners.

These little things often indicate most clearly the state of men's hearts. Suppose your servant were to say, " I cannot do this," or " I cannot do that," because it interferes with his personal ease and comfort. He cannot do this because he likes to sit on a cushion and work. Or he cannot do that because it would separate him from his family an hour and a half. What I is that doing service? When a man enters into service he gives up his ease and comfort for the interest and at the will of his employer. Is it true that any man is supremely devoted to the service of God, when he shows that his own ease and comfort are dearer than the kingdom of Jesus Christ, and that he would sooner sacrifice the salvation of sinners than sit on a hard seat, or be separated from his family an hour or two?

6. Those are serving their own gods, who give their time and money, when they do give, grudgingly, by constraint, and not of a ready mind, and with a cheerful heart.

What would you think of your servant, if you had to dun or drive him all the time, to do anything for your interest? Would you not say he was an eye-servant? How many people there are, who when they do anything on account of religion, do it grudgingly. If they do anything, it comes hard. If you go to one of these characters, and want his time or his money for any religious object it is difficult to get him engaged. It seems to go across the grain and is not easy or natural. It is plain he does not consider the interests of Christ's kingdom the same with his own. He may make a show of fearing the Lord, but he " serves " some other gods of his own.

7. Those who are always ready to ask how little they may do for religion rather than how much they may do, are serving their own gods.

There are multitudes of persons who seem always to ask how little they can get along with in what they do for God. You hear such a man making up his accounts of profit and loss—" So much made this year—then so much it costs for charity—so much obliged to give for religion " (OBLIGED to give for the interests of religion !)—" and so much lost by fire, and so much by bad debts," and so on.

is that man serving God ? It is a simple matter of fact that you have never set your hearts on the object of promoting religion in the world. If you had, you would ask, How much *can* I do for this object and for that ? Cannot I do so much—or so *much*—or *so much ?*

8. They who are laying up wealth for their families, to elevate and aggrandize them, are serving gods of their own, and not Jehovah.

Those who are thus aiming to elevate their own families into a different sphere, by laying up wealth for them, show that they have some other object to live for than bringing this world under the authority of Jesus Christ. They have other gods to serve. They may pretend to fear the Lord, but they "serve" their own gods.

9. Those who are making it their object to accumulate so much property that they can retire from business and live at ease, are serving their own gods.

There are many persons who profess to be the servants of God, but are eagerly engaged in gathering property, and calculating to retire to their country seat by-and-by, and live at their ease. What do you mean ? Has God given you a right to a perpetual Sabbath, as soon as you have made so much money ? Did God tell you, when you professed to enter his service, to work hard so many years, and then you might have a perpetual holiday ? Did he promise to excuse you after that from making the most of your time and talents, and let you live at ease the rest of your days ? If your thoughts are set upon this notion, I tell you, you are not serving God but your own selfishness and sloth.

10. Those persons are serving their own gods who would sooner gratify their appetites than deny themselves things that are unnecessary, or even hurtful, for the sake of doing good.

You find persons that greatly love things that do them

no good, and others even form an artificial appetite for a thing positively loathsome, and after it they will go, and no arguments will prevail upon them to abandon it for the sake of doing good. Are such persons absorbed in the service of God ? Certainly not. Will they sacrifice their lives for the kingdom of God ? Why you cannot make them even give up a quid of tobacco ! a weed that is injurious to health and loathsome to society ; they cannot give it up, were it to save a soul from death !

Who does not see that selfishness predominates in such persons ? It shows the astonishing strength of selfishness. You often see the strength of selfishness showing itself in some such little thing more than in things that are greater. The real state of a man's mind stands out, that self-gratification is the law of his life, so strongly, that it will not give place, even in a trifle, to those great interests, for which he ought to be willing to lay down his life.

11. Those persons who are most readily moved to action by appeals to their own selfish interests, show that they are serving their own gods.

You see what motive influences such a man. Suppose I wish to get him to subscribe for building a church, what must I urge ? Why, I must show how it will improve the value of his property, or advance his party, or gratify his selfishness in some other way. If he is more excited by these motives, than he is by a desire to save perishing souls and advance the kingdom of Christ, you see that he has never given himself up to serve the Lord. He is still serving himself. He is more influenced by his selfish interests than by all those benevolent principles on which all religion turns. The character of a true servant of God is right opposite to this.

Take the case of two servants, one devoted to his master's interests, and the other having no conscience or concern but to secure his wages. Go to one, and he throws into the shade all personal considerations, and enlists with heart and soul in achieving the object. The other will not act unless you present some selfish motive ; unless you say, "Do so, and I will raise your wages or set you up in business," or the like. Is there not a radical difference between these two servants ? Is not this an illustration of what actually takes place in our churches ? Propose a plan of doing good that will cost nothing, and they will all go for it. But propose a plan which is going to affect their personal interest—to cost money, or take up time in a busy season, and you will see they begin to divide. Some hesitate; some doubt ; some raise objections ; and some resolutely refuse. Some enlist at once, because they see it will do great good. Others stand back till you devise some means to excite their selfishness in its favor. What causes the difference ? Some of them are serving their own gods.

12. Those are of this character, who are more interested in other subjects than in religion.

If you find them more ready to talk on other subjects, more easily excited by them, more awake to learn the news, they are serving their own gods. What multitudes are more excited by the bank question, or the question about war, or about the fire, or anything of a worldly nature, than about revivals, missions, or anything connected with the interests of religion. You find them all engaged about politics or speculation ; but if you bring up the subject of religion,—ah, they are afraid of excitement ! and talk about animal feeling !—showing that religion is not the subject that is nearest their hearts. A man is always most easily excited on that subject that lies nearest his heart. Bring that up, and he is interested. When you can talk early and late about the news and other worldly topics, and when you cannot possibly be interested in the subject of religion, you know that your heart is not in it ; and if **you pretend to be a servant of God, you are a hypocrite.**

13. When persons are more jealous for their own fame than for God's glory, it shows that they live for themselves, and serve their own gods.

You see a man more vexed or grieved by what is said against him than against God ; whom does he serve ?—who is his God, himself or Jehovah ? There is a minister thrown into a fever because somebody has said a word derogatory to his scholarship, or his dignity, or his infallibility, while he is as cool as ice at all the indignities thrown upon the blessed God. Is that man a follower of Paul, willing to be considered a fool for the cause of Christ ? Did that man ever take the first lesson in religion ? If he had, he would rejoice to have his name cast out as evil for the cause of religion. No, he is not serving God ; he is serving his own gods.

14. Those are serving their own gods, who are not making the salvation of souls the great and leading object of their lives.

The end of all religious institutions, that which gives value to them all, is the salvation of sinners. The end for which Christ lives, and for which he has left his church in the world, is the salvation of sinners. This is the business which God sets his servants about, and if any man be not doing this, as his business—as the leading and main object of his life, he is not serving Jehovah, he is serving his own gods.

15. Those who are doing but little for God, or who bring but little to pass for God, cannot properly be said to serve him.

Suppose you ask a professed servant of God. "What are you doing for God ? Are you bringing anything to pass ? Are you instrumental in the conversion of any sinners ? Are you making impressions in favor of religion, or helping forward the cause of Christ ?" He replies, "Why I do not know,—I have a hope ; I sometimes think

I do love God ; but I do not know that I am doing anything in particular at present." Is that man serving God ?
—or is he serving his own gods ? "I talk to sinners sometimes," he says, "but they do not seem to feel much."
Then YOU do not feel. If your heart be not in it, no
wonder you cannot make sinners feel. Whereas, if you
do your duty, with your heart in the work, sinners cannot
help feeling.

16. Those who seek for happiness in religion, rather
than for usefulness, are serving their own gods.

Their religion is entirely selfish. They want to enjoy
religion, and are all the while inquiring how they can get
happy frames of mind, and how they can be pleasurably
excited in religious exercises. And they will go only to
such meetings, and sit only under such preaching, as will
make them happy ; never asking the question whether
that is the way to do the most good or not. Now, suppose
your servant should do so, and be constantly contriving
how to enjoy himself, and if he thought he could be most
happy in the parlor, stretched on the sofa, with a pillow
of down under his head, and another servant to fan him,
refusing to do the work which you set him about, and
which your interest urgently requires ; instead of manifesting a desire to work for you, and a solicitude for your
interest, and a willingness to lay himself out with all his
powers in your service, he wants only to be happy ! It is
just so with those professed servants of Jehovah, who want
to do nothing but sit on their handsome cushion, and have
their minister feed them. Instead of seeking how to do
good, they are only seeking to be happy. Their daily
prayer is not, like that of the converted Saul of Tarsus,
"Lord what wilt thou have me to do ?" but, "Lord, tell
me how I can be happy." Is that the spirit of Jesus
Christ ? No, he said, "I delight to do thy will. O God."
Is that the spirit of the apostle Paul ? No, he threw off

his upper garments at once, and made his arms bare for the field of labor.

17. Those who make their own salvation their supreme object in religion, are serving their own gods.

There are multitudes in the church, who show by their conduct, and even avow in their language, that their leading object is to secure their own salvation, and their grand determination is to get their own souls planted on the firm battlements of the heavenly Jerusalem, and walk the golden fields of Canaan above. If the Bible is not in error all such characters will go to hell. Their religion is pure selfishness. And " he that will save his life shall lose it, and he that will lose his life for my sake, shall save it."

CONCLUSION

1. See why so little is accomplished in the world for Jesus Christ.

It is because there are so few that do anything for it. It is because Jesus Christ has so few real servants in the world. How many professors do you suppose there are in this church, or in your whole acquaintance, that are really at work for God, and making a business of religion, and laying themselves out to advance the kingdom of Christ ? The reason why religion advances no faster is, that there are so few to advance it, and so many to hinder it. You see a parcel of people at a fire, trying to get out the goods of a store. Some are determined to get out the goods, but the rest are not engaged about it, and they divert their attention by talking about other things, or positively hinder them by finding fault with their way of doing it, or by holding them back. So it is in the church. Those who are desirous of doing the work are greatly hindered by the backwardness, the cavils, and the positive resistance of the rest.

2. See why so few Christians have the spirit of prayer.

How can they have the spirit of prayer ? What should God give them the spirit of prayer for ? Suppose a man engaged in his worldly schemes, and that God should give that man the spirit of prayer. Of course he would pray for that which lies nearest his heart ; that is, for success in his worldly schemes, to serve his own gods with. Will God give him the spirit of prayer for such purposes ?— Never. Let him go to his own gods for a spirit of prayer, out let him not expect Jehovah to bestow the spirit of prayer, while he is serving his own gods.

3. You see that there are a multitude of professors of religion that have not begun to be religious yet.

Said a man to one of them, Do you feel that your property and your business are all God's, and do you hold and manage them for God ? "O, no, " said he, "I have not got so far as that yet." Not got so far as that ! That man had been a professor of religion for years, and yet had not got so far as to consider his property, and busi ness, and all that he had, as belonging to God ! No doubt he was serving his own gods. For I insist upon it, that this is the very beginning of religion. What is conversion, but turning from the service of the world to the service of God ? And yet this man had not found out that he was God's servant. And he seemed to think he was getting a great way in religion, to feel that all he had was the Lord's.

4. It is great dishonesty for persons to profess to serve the Lord, and yet in reality serve themselves.

Yon who are performing religious duties from selfish motives are in reality trying to make God your servant. If your own interest be the supreme object, all your relig ious services are only desires to induce God to promote your interests. Why do you pray, or keep the Sabbath, or give your property for religious objects ? You answer,

"For the sake of promoting my own salvation." Indeed!
Not to glorify God, but to get to heaven! Do not you
think the devil would do all that, if he thought he could
gain his end by it—and be a devil still? The highest
style of selfishness must be to get God with all his attributes, enlisted in the service of your mighty self.

And now, my hearers, where are you all? Are you
serving Jehovah, or are you serving your own gods? How
have you been doing these six months that I have been ab-
sent? Have you done anything for God? Have you been
living as servants of God? Is Satan's kingdom weakened
by what you have done? Could you say now, "Come
with me, and I will show you this and that sinner converted, or this and that backslider reclaimed, or this and
that weak saint strengthened and aided?" Could you
bring living witnesses of what you have done in the service
of God? Or would your answer be, "I have been to meeting regularly on the Sabbath, and heard a great deal of
good preaching, and I have generally attended the prayer
meetings, and we had some precious meetings, and I have
prayed in my family, and twice or thrice a day in my
closet, and read the Bible." And in all that you have
been merely passive, as to anything done for God. You
have feared the Lord, and served your own gods.

"Yes, but I have sold so many goods, and made so
much money, of which I intend to give a tenth to the missionary cause." Who hath required this at your hand,
instead of saving souls? Going to send the gospel to the
heathen, and letting sinners right under your own eyes go
down to hell! Be not deceived. If you loved souls, if
you were engaged to serve God, you would think of souls
here, and do the work of God here. What should we
think of a missionary going to the heathen, who had never
said a word to sinners around him at home? Does he
love souls? There is burlesque in the idea of sending such

a man to the heathen. The man that will do nothing at home is not fit to go to the heathen. And he that pretends to be getting money for missions while he will not try to save sinners here, is an outrageous hypocrite.

3

DOUBTFUL ACTIONS ARE SINFUL

"He that doubteth is damned if he eat, because he eateth not of faith; for whatsoever is not of faith is sin." Romans 14:23.

IT was a custom among the idolatrous heathen to offer the bodies of slain beasts in sacrifice. A part of every beast that was offered belonged to the priest. The priests used to send their portion to market to sell, and it was sold in the shambles as any other meat. The Christian Jews that were scattered everywhere were very particular as to what meats they ate, so as not even to run the least danger of violating the Mosaic law, and they raised doubts, and created disputes and difficulties among the churches. This was one of the subjects about which the church of Corinth was divided and agitated, until they finally wrote to the apostle Paul for directions. A part of the First Epistle to the Corinthians was doubtless written as a reply to such inquiries. It seems there were some who carried their scruples so far that they thought it not proper to eat any meat ; for if they went to market for it, they were continually in danger of buying that which was offered to idols. Others thought it made no difference ; they had a right to eat meat, and they would buy it in the market as they found it, and give themselves no trouble about the matter. To quell the dispute, they wrote to Paul, and in chapter viii, he takes up the subject and discusses it in full.

" Now, as touching things offered unto idols, we know that we all have knowledge. Knowledge puffeth up, but charity edifieth. And if any man think that he knoweth anything, he knoweth nothing yet as he ought to know. But if any man love God, the same is known of him. As concerning therefore the eating of those things that are offered in sacrifice unto idols, we know that an idol is nothing in the world, and that there is none other God but one. For though there be that are called gods, whether in heaven or in earth, (as there be gods many, and lords many,) but to us there is but one God, the Father, of whom are all things, and we in him ; and one Lord Jesus Christ, by whom are all things, and we by him. Howbeit there is not in every man that knowledge ; for some with conscience of the idol unto this hour eat it as a thing offered unto an idol ; and their conscience, being weak, is defiled.

" His conscience is defiled," that is, he regards it as a meat offered to an idol, and is really practising idolatry The eating of meat is a matter of total indifference, in itself.

" But meat commendeth us not to God ; for neither if we eat are we the better ; neither if we eat not, are we the worse. But take heed lest by any means this liberty of yours become a stumbling block to them that are weak. For if any man see thee, which hast knowledge, sit at meat in the idol's temple, shall not the conscience of him which is weak be emboldened to eat those things offered to idols ; and through thy knowledge shall the weak brother perish for whom Christ died ? "

Although they might have a sufficient knowledge on the subject to know that an idol is nothing, and cannot make any change in the meat itself, yet if they should be seen eating meat that was known to have been offered to an idol, those who were weak might be emboldened by it to eat the sacrifices as such, or as an act of worship to the idol, supposing all the while that they were but following the example of their more enlightened brethren.

But when ye sin so against the brethren, and wound their weak conscience, ye sin against Christ. " Wherefore, if meat make my brother to offend, I will eat no more flesh while the world standeth, lest I make my brother to offend."

This is his benevolent conclusion, that he would rather forego the use of flesh altogether than be the occasion of drawing a weak brother away into idolatry. For, in fact, to sin so against a weak brother is to sin against Christ.

In writing to the Romans he takes up the same subject—the same dispute had existed there. After laying down some general maxims and principles, he gives this rule :

"Him that is weak in faith receive ye, but not to doubtful disputation. For one believeth that he may eat all things ; another who is weak, eateth herbs."

There were some among them who chose to live entirely on vegetables, rather than run the risk of buying in the shambles flesh which had been offered in sacrifice to idols. Others ate their flesh as usual, buying what was offered in market, asking no questions for conscience' sake. Those who lived on vegetables charged the others with idolatry. And those that ate flesh accused the others of superstition and weakness. This was wrong.

"Let not him that eateth, despise him that eateth not ; and let not him which eateth not, judge him that eateth ; for God hath received him. Who art thou that judgest another man's servant ? to his own master he standeth or falleth ; yea, he shall be holden up ; for God is able to make him stand."

There was also a controversy about observing the Jewish festival days and holy days. A part supposed that God required this, and therefore they observed them. The others neglected them because they supposed God did not require the observance.

"One man esteemeth one day above another ; another esteemeth every day alike. Let every man be fully persuaded in his own mind. He that regardeth the day, regardeth it unto the Lord ; and he that regardeth not the day, to the Lord he doth not regard it. He that eateth, eateth to the Lord, for he giveth God thanks ; and he that eateth not, to the Lord he eateth not, and giveth God thanks. For none of us liveth to himself, and no man dieth to himself. For whether we live, we live unto the Lord ; and whether we die, we die unto the Lord : whether we live therefore, or die, we are the Lord's. For to this end Christ both died, and rose, and revived, that he might be Lord both of the dead and living. But why dost thou judge thy brother ? or why dost thou set at nought thy brother ? for we shall all stand before the judgment-seat of Christ. For as it is written, As I live, saith the Lord, every knee shall bow to me, and every tongue shall confess to God. So then every one of us shall give account of himself to God. Let us not therefore, judge one another any more : but judge this rather, that no man put a stumbling-block, or an occasion to fall in his brother's way."

Now mark what he says.

" But if thy brother be grieved with thy meat, now walkest thou not charitably : destroy not him with thy meat, for whom Christ died."

That is, I know that the distinction of meats into clean and unclean, is not binding under Christ, but to him that believes in the distinction, it is a crime to eat indiscriminately, because he does what he believes to be contrary to the commands of God. " All things indeed are pure, but it is evil to him that eateth with offence." Every man should be persuaded in his own mind, that what he is doing is right. If a man eat of meats called unclean, not being clear in his mind that it is right, he offends God.

" It is good neither to eat flesh, nor to drink wine, nor

any thing whereby thy brother stumbleth, or is offended, or is made weak."

This is a very useful hint to those wine-bibbers and beer-guzzlers, who think the cause of temperance is going to be ruined by giving up wine and beer, when it is notorious, to every person of the least observation, that these things are the greatest hinderance to the cause all over the country.

"Hast thou faith ? have it to thyself before God. Happy is he that condemneth not himself in THAT thing which he alloweth. And he that doubteth is damned if he eat, because he eateth not of faith ; for whatsoever is not of faith is sin."

The word rendered damned means condemned, or adjudged guilty of breaking the law of God. If a man doubts whether it is lawful to do a thing, and while in that state of doubt, he does it, he displeases God, he breaks the law and is condemned whether the thing be in itself right or wrong. I have been thus particular in explaining the text in its connection with the context, because I wished fully to satisfy your minds of the correctness of the principle laid down—That if a man does that of which he doubts the lawfulness, he sins, and is condemned for it in the sight of God.

Whether it is lawful itself, is not the question. If he doubts its lawfulness, it is wrong in him.

There is one exception which ought to be noticed here, and that is, where a man as honestly and fully doubts the lawfulness of omitting to do it as he does the lawfulness of doing it. President Edwards meets this exactly in his 39th resolution :

"Resolved, never to do any thing that I so much question the lawfulness of, as that I intend, at the same time, to consider and examine afterwards, whether it be lawful or not : except I as much question the lawfulness of the omission."

A man may have equal doubts whether he is bound to do a thing or not to do it. Then all that can be said is, that he must act according to the best light he can get. But where he doubts the lawfulness of the act, but has no cause to doubt the lawfulness of the omission, and yet does it, he sins and is condemned before God, and must repent or be damned. In further examination of the subject, I propose,

I. To show some reasons why a man is criminal for doing that of which he doubts the lawfulness.

II. To show its application to a number of specific cases.

III. Offer a few inferences and remarks, as time may allow.

I. I am to show some reasons for the correctness of the principle laid down in the text—that if a man does that of which he doubts the lawfulness, he is condemned.

1. One reason why an individual is condemned if he does that of which he doubts the lawfulness, is—That if God so far enlightens his mind as to make him doubt the lawfulness of an act, he is bound to stop there and examine the question and settle it to his satisfaction.

To illustrate this : suppose your child is desirous of doing a certain thing, or suppose he is invited by his companions to go somewhere, and he doubts whether you would be willing, do you not see that it is his duty to ask you ? If one of his schoolmates invites him home, and he doubts whether you would like it, and yet goes, is not this palpably wrong ?

Or suppose a man cast away on a desolate island, where he finds no human being, and he takes up his abode in a solitary cave, considering himself as all alone and destitute of friends, or relief, or hope ; but every morning he finds a supply of nutritious and wholesome food prepared for him, and set by the mouth of his cave, sufficient for his wants that day.   What is his duty ?   Do you say, he does not know that there is a being on the island, and therefore he is not under obligations to any one ?   Does not gratitude, on the other hand, require him to search and find out his unseen friend, and thank him for his kindness ? He cannot say, " I doubt whether there is any being here, and therefore will do nothing but eat my allowance and take my ease, and care for nothing."   His not searching for his benefactor would of itself convict him of as desperate wickedness of heart, as if he knew who it was, and refused to return thanks for the favors received.

Or suppose an Atheist opens his eyes on this blessed light of heaven, and breathes this air, sending health and vigor through his frame.   Here is evidence enough of the being of God to set him on the inquiry after that Great Being who provides all these means of life and happiness. And if he does not inquire for farther light, if he does not care, if he sets his heart against God, he shows that he has the heart as well as the intellect of an Atheist.   He has, to say the least, evidence that there MAY BE a God. What then is his business ?   Plainly, it is to set himself honestly, and with a most child-like and reverent spirit, to inquire after him and pay him reverence.   If, when he has so much light as to doubt whether there may not be a God, he still goes around as if there were none, and does not inquire for truth and obey it, he shows that his heart is wrong, and that it says let there be no God.

There is a Deist, and here a book claiming to be a revelation from God.   Many good men have believed it to be so.   The evidences are such as to have perfectly satisfied the most acute and upright minds of its truth.   The evidences, both external and internal are of great weight. To say there are NO evidences is itself enough to bring any man's soundness of mind into question, or his honesty. There is, to say the least that can be said, sufficient evidence to create a doubt whether it is a fable and an imposture.   This is in fact but a small part, but we will take it on this ground.   Now is it his duty to reject it?   No Deist pretends that he can be so fully persuaded in his own mind, as to be free from all doubt.   All he dares to attempt is to raise cavils and create doubts on the other side.   Here, then, it is his duty to stop, and not oppose the Bible, until he can prove without a doubt, that it is not from God.

So with the Unitarian.   Granting (what is by no means true) that the evidence in the Bible is not sufficient to remove all doubts that Jesus Christ is God ; yet it affords evidence enough to raise a doubt on the other side, and he has no right to reject the doctrine as untrue, but is bound humbly to search the scriptures and satisfy himself.   Now, no intelligent and honest man can say that the scriptures afford " no evidence " of the divinity of Christ.   They do afford evidence which has convinced and fully satisfied thousands of the acutest minds, and who have before been opposed to the doctrine.   No man can reject the doctrine without a doubt, because here is evidence that it may be true.   And if it may be true, and there is reason to doubt, if it is not true, then he rejects it at his peril.

Then the Universalist.   Where is one who can say he has not so much as a doubt whether there is not a hell, where sinners go after death into endless torment.   He is bound to stop and inquire, and search the scriptures.   It is not enough for him to say he does not believe in a hell. It may be there is, and if he rejects it, and goes on reckless of the truth whether there is or not, that itself makes him a rebel against God.   He doubts whether there is not a hell which he ought to avoid, and yet he acts as if he was certain and had no doubts.   He is condemned.   I once knew a physician who was a Universalist, and who has gone to eternity to try the reality of his speculations.   He once told me that he had strong doubts of the truth of Universalism, and had mentioned his doubts to a minister, who confessed that he, too, doubted its truth, and he did not believe there was a Universalist in the world who did not.

2. For a man to do a thing when he doubts whether it is lawful shows that he is selfish, and has other objects besides doing the will of God.

It shows that he wants to do it to gratify himself. He doubts whether God will approve of it, and yet he does it. Is he not a rebel? If he honestly wished to serve God, when he doubted he would stop and inquire and examine until he was satisfied. But to go forward while he is in doubt, shows that he is selfish and wicked, and is willing to do it whether God is pleased or not, and that he wants to do it, whether it is right or wrong. He does it because he wants to do it, and not because it is right.

3. To act thus is an impeachment of the divine goodness.

He assumes it as uncertain whether God has given a sufficient revelation of his will, so that he might know his duty if he would. He virtually says that the path of duty is left so doubtful that he must decide at a venture.

4. It indicates slothfulness and stupidity of mind.

It shows that he had rather act wrong than use the necessary diligence to learn and know the path of duty. It shows that he is either negligent or dishonest in his inquiries.

5. It manifests a reckless spirit.

It shows a want of conscience, an indifference to right, a setting aside of the authority of God, a disposition not to do God's will, and not to care whether He is pleased or displeased, a desperate recklessness and headlong temper, that is the height of wickedness.

The principle then, which is so clearly laid down, in

the text and context, and also in the chapter which I read from Corinthians, is fully sustained by examination—That for a man to do a thing, when he doubts the lawfulness of it, is sin, for which he is condemned before God, and must repent or be damned.

II.   I am now to show the application of this principle to a variety of particular cases in human life.   But,

First—I will mention some cases where a person may be equally in doubt with respect to the lawfulness of a thing, whether he is bound to do it or not to do it.

Take the subject of Wine at the Communion Table.

Since the temperance reformation has brought up the question about the use of wine, and various wines have been analyzed and the quantity of alcohol they contain has been disclosed, and the difficulty shown of getting wines in this country that are not highly alcoholic, it has been seriously doubted by some whether it is right to use such wines as we can get here in celebrating the Lord's supper.   Some are strong in the belief that wine is an essential part of the ordinance, and that we ought to use the best wine we can get, and there leave the matter.   Others say that we ought not to use alcoholic or intoxicating wine at all ; and that as wine is not, in their view, essential to the ordinance, it is better to use some other drink.   Both these classes are undoubtedly equally conscientious, and desirous to do what they have most reason to believe is agreeable to the will of God.   And others, again, are in doubt on the matter.   I can easily conceive that some conscientious persons may be very seriously in doubt which way to act.   They are doubtful whether it is right to use alcoholic wine, and are doubtful whether it is right to use any other drink in the sacrament.   Here is a case that comes under President Edwards' rule, " where it is doubtful in my mind, whether I ought to do it or not to do it," and which men must decide according to the best light they can get, honestly, and with a single desire to know and do what is most pleasing to God.

I do not intend to discuss this question, of the use of wine at the communion, nor is this the proper place for a full examination of the subject. I introduced it now merely for the purpose of illustration. But since it is before us, I will make two or three remarks.

(1.) I have never apprehended so much evil as some do, from the use of common wine at the communion. I have not felt alarmed at the danger or evil of taking a sip of wine, a teaspoonful or so, once a month, or once in two months, or three months. I do not believe that the disease of intemperance (and intemperance, you know, is in reality a disease of the body) will be either created or continued by so slight a cause. Nor do I believe it is going to injure the temperance cause so much as some have supposed. And therefore, where a person uses wine as we have been accustomed to do, and is fully persuaded in his own mind, he does not sin.

(2.) On the other hand, I do not think that the use of wine is any way essential to the ordinance. Very much has been said and written and printed on the subject, which has darkened counsel by words without knowledge. To my mind there are stronger reasons than I have anywhere seen exhibited, for supposing that wine is not essential to this ordinance. Great pains have been taken to prove that our Saviour used wine that was unfermented, when he instituted the supper, and which therefore contained no alcohol. Indeed, this has been the point chiefly in debate, But in fact it seems just as irrelevant as it would to discuss the question, whether he used wheat or oaten bread, or whether it was leavened or unleavened. Why do we not hear *this* question vehemently discussed ? Because all regard it as unessential.

In order to settle this question about the wine, we

should ask what is the meaning of the ordinance of the supper. What did our Saviour design to do ? It was to take the two staple articles for the support of life, food and drink, and use them to represent the necessity and virtue of the atonement.

It is plain that Christ had that view of it, for it corresponds with what he says, "My flesh is meat indeed, and my blood is drink indeed." So he poured out water in the temple, and said, "If any man thirst, let him come unto me and drink." He is called the "Bread of life." Thus it was customary to show the value of Christ's sufferings by food and drink. Why did he take bread instead of some other article of food ? Those who know the history and usages of that country will see that he chose that article of food which was in most common use among the people. When I was in Malta, it seemed as if a great part of the people lived on bread alone. They would go in crowds to the market place, and buy each a piece or coarse bread, and stand and eat it. Thus the most common and the most universally wholesome article of diet is chosen by Christ to represent his flesh. Then why did he take wine to drink ? For the same reason ; wine is the common drink of the people, especially at their meals, in all those countries. It is sold there for about a cent a bottle, wine being cheaper than small beer is here. In Sicily I was informed that wine was sold for five cents a gallon, and I do not know but it was about as cheap as water. And you will observe that the Lord's supper was first observed at the close of the feast of the passover, at which the Jews always used wine. The meaning of the Saviour in this ordinance, then, is this :—As food and drink are essential to the life of the body, so his body and blood, or his atonement, are essential to the life of the soul. For myself, I am fully convinced that wine is not essential to the communion, and I should not hesitate to give water to any individual who conscientiously preferred it. Let it be the common food and drink of the country, the support of life to the body, and it answers the end of the institution. If I was a missionary among the Esquimaux Indians, where they live on dried seal's flesh and snow-water, I would administrate the supper in those substances. It would convey to their minds the idea that they cannot live without Christ.

I say, then, that if an individual is fully persuaded in his own mind, he does not sin in giving up the use of wine. Let this church be fully persuaded in their own minds, and I shall have no scruple to do either way, if they will substitute any other wholesome drink, that is in common use, instead of the wine. And at the same time, I have no objection myself against going on in the old way.

Now, do not lose sight of the great principle that is under discussion. It is this : where a man doubts honestly, whether it is lawful to do a thing, and doubts equally, on the other hand whether it is lawful to omit doing it, he must pray over the matter, and search the scriptures, and get the best light he can on the subject, and then act. And when he does this, he is by no means to be judged or censured by others for the course he takes. "Who art thou that judgest another man's servant?" And no man is authorized to make his own conscience the rule of his neighbor's conduct.

A similar case is where a minister is so situated that it is necessary for him to go a distance on the Sabbath to preach, as where he preaches to two congregations, and the like. Here he may honestly doubt what is his duty, on both hands. If he goes he appears to strangers to disregard the Sabbath. If he does not go, the people will have no preaching. The direction is, let him search the scriptures, and get the best light he can, make it a subject of prayer, weigh it thoroughly, and act according to his best judgment.

So in the case of a Sabbath-school teacher. He may live at a distance from the school, and be obliged to travel to it on the Sabbath, or they will have no school. And he may honestly doubt which is his duty, to remain in his own church on the Sabbath, or to travel there, five, eight, or ten miles, to a destitute neighborhood, to keep up the Sabbath school. Here he must decide for himself, according to the best light he can get. And let no man set himself up to judge over a humble and conscientious disciple of the Lord Jesus.

You see that in all these cases it is understood and is plain that the design is to honor God, and the sole ground of doubt is, which course will really honor him. Paul says, in reference to all laws of this kind, " He that regardeth the day, regardeth it unto the Lord ; and he that regardeth not the day, to the Lord he doth not regard it." The design is to do right, and the doubt is as to the means of doing it in the best manner.

Secondly—I will mention some cases, where the DESIGN is wrong, where the object is to gratify self, and the individual has doubts whether he may do it lawfully. I shall refer to cases concerning which there is a difference of opinion—to acts of which the least that can be said is that a man must have doubts of their being lawful.

1. Take, for instance, the making and vending of alcoholic drinks.

After all that has been said on this subject, and all the light that has been thrown upon the question, is there a man living in this land who can say he sees no reason to doubt the lawfulness of this business. To say the least that can be said, there can be no honest mind but must be brought to doubt it. We suppose, indeed, that there is no honest mind but must know it is unlawful and criminal.

But take the most charitable supposition possible for tha distiller or the vender, and suppose he is not fully convinced of its unlawfulness. We say he must, at least, DOUBT its lawfulness. What is he to do then? Is he to shut his eyes to the light, and go on, regardless of truth, so long as he can keep from seeing it? No. He may cavil and raise objections as much as he pleases, but he knows that he has doubts about the lawfulness of his business; and if he doubts, and still persists in doing it, without taking the trouble to examine and see what is right, he is just as sure to be damned as if he went on in the face of knowledge. You hear these men say, "Why, I am not fully persuaded in my own mind that the Bible forbids making or vending ardent spirits." Well, suppose you are not fully convinced, suppose all your possible and conceivable objections and cavils are not removed, what then? You know you have doubts about its lawfulness. And it is not necessary to take such ground to convict you of doing wrong. If you doubt its lawfulness, and yet persist in doing it, you are in the way to hell.

2. So where an individual is engaged in an employment that requires him to break the Sabbath.

As for instance, attending on a post-office that is opened on the Sabbath, or a turnpike gate, or in a steam-boat, or any other employment that is not work of necessity. There are always some things that must be done on the Sabbath, they are works of absolute necessity or of mercy.

But suppose a case in which the labor is not necessary, as in the transportation of the mail on the Sabbath, or the like? The least that can be said, the lowest ground that can be taken by charity itself, without turning fool, is, that the lawfulness of such employment is doubtful. And if they persist in doing it, they sin, and are on the way to hell. God has sent out the penalty of his law against them, and if they do not repent they must be damned.

3. Owning stocks in steamboat and railroad companies, in stages, canal boats, etc., that break the Sabbath.

Can any such owner truly say he does not doubt the lawfulness of such-an investment of capital ? Can charity stoop lower than to say, that man must strongly doubt whether such labor is a work of necessity or mercy ? It is not necessary in the case to demonstrate that it is unlawful—though that can be done fully, but only to show so much light as to create a doubt of its lawfulness. Then if he persist in doing it, with that doubt unsatisfied, he is condemned—and lost.

4. The same remarks will apply to all sorts of lottery gambling. He doubts.

5. Take the case of those indulgences of appetite which are subject of controversy, and which, to say the least, are of doubtful right.

(1.) The drinking of wine, and beer, and other fermented intoxicating liquors. In the present aspect of the temperance cause, is it not questionable at least, whether making use of these drinks is not transgressing the rule laid down by the apostle, " It is good neither to eat flesh nor drink wine, nor anything whereby thy brother stumbleth, or is offended, or made weak." No man can make me believe he has no doubts of the lawfulness of doing it. There is no certain proof of its lawfulness, and there is strong proof of its unlawfulness, and every man who does it while he doubts the lawfulness, is condemned, and if he persists, is damned.

If there is any sophistry in all this, I should like to know it, for I do not wish to deceive others nor to be deceived myself. But I am entirely deceived if this is not a simple, direct, and necessary inference, from the sentiment of the text.

(2.) Tobacco. Can any man pretend that he has no doubt that it is agreeable to the will of God for him to use tobacco ? No man can pretend that he doubts the lawfulness of his OMISSION of these things. Does any man living think that he is bound in duty to make use of wine, or strong beer, or tobacco, as a luxury ? No. The doubt is all on one side. What shall we say then, of that man who doubts the lawfulness of it, and still fills his face with the poisonous weed ? He is condemned.

(3.) I might refer to tea and coffee. It is known generally, that these substances are not nutritious at all, and that nearly eight millions of dollars are spent annually for them in this country. Now, will any man pretend that he does not doubt the lawfulness of spending all this money for that which is of no use, and which are *well known* to all who have examined the subject, to be positively injurious, intolerable to weak stomachs, and as much as the strongest can dispose of ? And all this while the various benevolent societies of the age are loudly calling for *help* to send the gospel abroad and save a world from hell ? To think of the church alone spending millions upon their tea tables—is there no doubt here ?

6. Apply this principle to various amusements.

(1.) The theatre. There are vast multitudes of professors of religion who attend the theatre. And they contend that the Bible no where forbids it. Now mark.— What Christian professor ever went to a theatre and did not doubt whether he was doing what was lawful. I by no means admit that it is a point which is only doubtful. I suppose it is a very plain case, and can be shown to be, that it is unlawful. But I am now only meeting those of you, if there are any here, who go to the theatre, and are trying to cover up yourselves in the refuge that the Bible nowhere expressly forbids it.

(2.) Parties of pleasure, where they go and eat and drink to surfeiting. Is there no reason to doubt whether that is such a use of time and money as God requires ?

Look at the starving poor, and consider the effect of this gaiety and extravagance, and see if you will ever go to another such party or make one, without doubting its lawfulness. Where can you find a man, or a woman, that will go so far as to say they have no doubt? Probably there is not one honest mind who will say this. And if you doubt, and still do it, you are condemned.

You see that this principle touches a whole class of things, about which there is a controversy, and where people attempt to parry off by saying it is not worse than to do so and so, and thus get away from the condemning sentence of God's law. But in fact, if there is a doubt, it is their duty to abstain.

(3.) Take the case of balls, of novel reading, and other methods of wasting time. Is this God's way to spend your lives? Can you say you have no doubt of it?

7. Making calls on the Sabbath. People will make a call, and then make an apology about it. "I did not know that it was quite right, but I thought I would venture it." He is a Sabbath-breaker in heart, at all events, because he doubts.

8. Compliance with worldly customs at new-year's day. Then the ladies are all at home, and the gentlemen are running all about town to call on them, and the ladies make their great preparations, and treat them with their cake, and their wine, and punch, enough to poison them almost to death, and all together are bowing down to the goddess of fashion. Is there a lady here that does not doubt the lawfulness of all this? I say it can be demonstrated to be wicked, but I only ask the ladies of this city, Is it not *doubtful* whether this is all lawful? I should call in question the sanity of the man or woman that had no doubt of the lawfulness of such a custom, in the midst of such prevailing intemperance as exists in this city. Who among you will practise it again? Practise it

if you dare—at the peril of your soul ! If you do that
which is merely doubtful, God frowns and condemns ; and
HIS voice must be regarded.

I know people try to excuse the matter, and say it is
well to have a day appropriated to such calls, when every
lady is at home and every gentleman freed from business,
and all that. And all that is very well. But when it is
seen to be so abused and to produce so much evil, I ask
every Christian here, if you can help doubting its lawfulness ? And if it be doubtful, it comes under the rule :
" If meat make my brother to offend." If keeping new-
years leads to so much gluttony, and drunkenness, and
wickedness, does it not bring the lawfulness of it into
doubt ? Yes, that is the least that can be said, and they
who doubt and yet do it, sin against God.

9. Compliance with the extravagant fashions of the day.

Christian lady ! have you never doubted, do you not
now doubt, whether it be lawful for you to copy these
fashions, brought from foreign countries, and from places
which it were a shame even to name in this assembly ?
Have you no doubt about it ? And if you doubt and do
it, you are condemned, and must repent of your sin, or you
will be lost forever !

10. Intermarriages of Christians with impenitent sinners.

This answer always comes up. " But after all you say,
it is not *certain* that these marriages are not lawful."
Supposing it be so, yet does not the Bible and the nature
of the case make it at least doubtful whether they are
right ? It can be demonstrated, indeed, to be unlawful.
But suppose it could not be reduced to demonstration ;
what Christain ever did it and did not doubt whether
it was lawful ? And he that doubteth is condemned.
See that christian man or woman that is about forming
such a connection—doubting all the way whether it is

right : trying to pray down conscience under pretext of praying for light : praying all around your duty, and yet pressing on. *Take care !* You know you doubt the lawfulness of what you propose, and remember that " he that doubteth is damned."

Thus you see, my hearers, that here is a principle that will stand by you when you attempt to rebuke sin, if the power of society be employed to face you down, or put you on the defensive, and demand absolute proof of the sinfulness of a cherished practice. Remember *the burden of proof does not lie on you,* to show beyond a doubt the absolute unlawfulness of the thing. If you can show sufficient reason to question its lawfulness, and to create a valid doubt whether it is according to the will of God, you shift the burden of proof to the other side. And unless they can remove the doubt, and show that there is no room for doubt, they have no right to continue in the doubtful practice, and if they do, they sin against God.

CONCLUSION

1. The knowledge of duty is not indispensable to moral obligation, but the possession of the means of knowledge is sufficient to make a person responsible.

If a man has the means of knowing whether it is right or wrong he is bound to use the means, and is bound to inquire and ascertain at his peril.

2. If those are condemned, and adjudged worthy of damnation, who do that of which they doubt the lawfulness, what shall we say of the multitudes who are doing continually that which they know and confess to be wrong ?

Woe to that man who practises that which he condemns. And "happy is he that condemneth not himself in that thing which he alloweth."

3. Hypocrites often attempt to shelter themselves behind their doubts to get clear of their duty.

The hypocrite is unwilling to be enlightened, he does not wish to know the truth, because he does not wish to obey the Lord, and so he hides behind his doubts, and turns away his eye from the light, and will not look or examine to see what his duty is, and in this way he tries to shield himself from responsibility. But God will drag them out from behind this refuge of lies, by the principle laid down in the text, that their very doubts condemn them.

Many will not be enlightened on the subject of tem perance, and still persist in drinking or selling rum, because they are not fully convinced it is wrong. And they will not read a tract or a paper, nor attend a temperance meeting, for fear they shall be convinced. Many are resolved to indulge in the use of wine and strong beer, and they will not listen to anything calculated to convince them of the wrong. It shows that they are determined to indulge in sin, and they hope to hide behind their doubts. What better evidence could they give that they are hypocrites?

Who, in all these United States, can say, that he has no doubt of the lawfulness of slavery? Yet the great body of the people will not hear anything on the subject, and they go into a passion if you name it, and it is even seriously proposed, both at the north and at the south, to pass laws forbidding inquiry and discussion on the subject. Now suppose these laws should be passed, for the purpose of enabling the nation to shelter itself behind its doubts whether slavery is a sin, that ought to be abolished immediately—will that help the matter? Not at all. If they continue to hold their fellow men as property, in slavery, while they doubt its lawfulness, they are condemned before God, and we may be sure their sin will find them out, and God will let them know how He regards it.

It is amazing to see the foolishness of people on this

subject ; as if by refusing to get clear of their doubts, they could get clear of their sin. Think of the people of the south : Christians, and even ministers, refusing to read a paper on the subject of slavery, and perhaps sending it back with abusive or threatening words. Threatening ! for what ? For reasoning with them about their duty ? It can be demonstrated absolutely, that slavery is unlawful, and ought to be repented of, and given up, like any other sin. But suppose they only doubt the lawfulness of slavery, and do not mean to be enlightened, they are condemned of God. Let them know that they cannot put this thing down, they cannot clear themselves of it. So long as they doubt its lawfulness, they cannot hold men in slavery without sin ; and that they do doubt its lawfulness is demonstrated by this opposition to discussion.

We may suppose a case, and perhaps there may be some such in the southern country, where a man doubts the lawfulness of holding slaves, and equally doubts the lawfulness of emancipating them in their present state of ignorance and dependence. In that case he comes under Pres. Edward's rule, and it is his duty not to fly in a passion with those who would call his attention to it, not to send back newspapers and refuse to read, but to inquire on all hands for light, and examine the question honestly in the light of the word of God, till his doubts are cleared up. The least he can do is to set himself with all his power to educate them and train them to take care of themselves as fast and as thoroughly as possible, and to put them in a state where they can be set at liberty.

4. It is manifest there is but very little conscience in the church.

See what multitudes are persisting to do what they strongly doubt the lawfulness of.

5. There is still less love to God than there is con science.

It cannot be pretended that love to God is the cause of all this following of fashions, this practising indulgences, and other things of which people doubt the lawfulness. They do not persist in these things because they love God so well. No, no, but they persist in it because they wish to do it, to gratify themselves, and they had rather run the risk of doing wrong than to have their doubts cleared up. It is because they have so little love for God, so little care for the honor of God.

6. Do not say, in your prayers, "O Lord, if I have sinned in this thing, O Lord, forgive me the sin."

If you have done that of which you doubted the lawfulness, you have sinned, whether the thing itself be right or wrong. And you must repent, and ask forgiveness.

And now, let me ask you all who are here present, are you convinced that to do what you doubt the lawfulness of, is sin? If you are, I have one more question to ask you. Will you from this time relinquish every thing of which you doubt the lawfulness? Every amusement, every indulgence, every practice, every pursuit? Will you do it, or will you stand before the solemn judgment seat of Jesus Christ, condemned? If you will not relinquish these things, you show that you are an impenitent sinner, and do not INTEND to obey God, and if you do not repent you bring down upon your head God's condemnation and wrath, for ever

4

TRUE SAINTS

"Who is on the Lord's side?" Exodus 32:26.

THE question was addressed by Moses to the professed people of God, immediately after their great departure from God while Moses was on the Mount, when they went and worshipped a golden calf which had been cast for them by Aaron. After expostulating with the guilty nation, he called out, " Who is on the Lord's side ? " It is not my intention to dwell on the history of this case particularly, but to come at once to the main design I have in view this evening, which is to show that there are

THREE CLASSES OF PROFESSING CHRISTIANS.

I. The true friends of God and man.

II. Those who are actuated by hope and fear, or in other words by self-love, or by selfishness.

III. Those who are actuated by public opinion.

These three classes may be known by attending to the characteristic developments which show what is the leading design in their religion. It needs not be proved, that persons may set out in religion from very different motives, some from real love to religion, and some from other motives. The differences·may be arranged in these three classes, and by attending to the development of their real design in becoming religious, you learn their characters. They all profess to be servants of God, and yet by observing the lives of many, it becomes manifest that instead of their being God's servants they are only trying to make God their servant. Their leading aim and object is to

secure their own salvation, or some other advantage for
themselves, through the medium of the favor of God.
They are seeking to make God their friend, that they may
make use of him to serve their own turn.

I. There is a class of professed Christians who are the
true friends of God and man.

If you attend to those things which develop the true
design and aim of their religion, you will see it to be such.
They are truly and sincerely benevolent.

1. They will make it manifest that this is their character, by their carefulness in avoiding sin.

They will show that they hate it in themselves, and that
they hate it in others. They will not justify it in themselves, and they will not justify it in others. They will
not seek to cover up or to excuse their own sins, neither
will they try to cover up or to excuse the sins of others.
In short they aim at *perfect holiness*. This course
of conduct makes it evident that they are the true
friends of God. I do not mean to say that every true
friend of God is perfect, no more than I would say that
every truly affectionate and obedient child is perfect, or
never fails in duty to his parent. But if he is an affectionate and obedient child, his aim is to obey always, and if
he fails in any respect, he by no means justifies it, or pleads
for it, or aims to cover it up, but as soon as he comes to
think of the matter, is dissatisfied with himself, and condemns his conduct.

So these persons who are the true friends of God and
man, are ever ready to complain of themselves, and to
blame and condemn themselves for what is wrong. But
you never see them finding fault with God. You never
hear them excusing themselves and throwing off the blame
upon their Maker, by telling of their inability to obey God,
or speaking as if God had required impossibilities of his
creatures. They always speak as if they felt that what

God has required is right and reasonable, and themselves only to blame for their disobedience.

2. They manifest a deep abhorrence of the sins of other people.

They do not cover up the sins of others, or plead for them and excuse them, or smooth them over by "perhaps this," or "perhaps that." You never hear them apologizing for sin. As they are indignant at sin in themselves, they are just as much so when they see it in others. They know its horrible nature, and abhor it always.

3. Another thing in which this spirit manifests itself, is zeal for the honor and glory of God.

They show the same ardor to promote God's honor and interest, that the true patriot does to promote the honor and interest of his country. If he greatly loves his country, its government, and its interest, he sets his heart upon promoting its advancement and benefit. He is never so happy as when he is doing something for the honor and advancement of his country. So a child that truly loves his father, is never so happy as when he is advancing his father's honor and interest. And he never feels more indignant grief, than when he sees his father abused or injured. If he sees his father disobeyed or abused by those who ought to obey, and love, and honor him, his heart breaks forth with indignant grief.

There are multitudes of professing Christians, and even ministers, who are very zealous to defend their own character and their own honor. But this one class feel more engaged, and their hearts beat higher, when defending or advancing God's honor. These are the friends of God and man.

4. They show that they *sympathize* with God in his feelings towards man.

They have the same kind of friendship for souls that God feels. I do not mean that they feel in the same de-

gree, but that they have the same kind of feelings. There
is such a thing as loving the souls of men and hating their
conduct too. There is such a thing as constitutional sympathy, which persons feel for those who are in distress.
This is natural. You always feel this for a person in distress, unless you have some selfish reason for feeling malev-
olent. If you saw a murderer hung, you would feel compassion for him. The wicked have this natural sympathy
for those that suffer.

There is another peculiar kind of sympathy which the
real child of God feels, and manifests towards sinners. It
is a mingled feeling of abhorrence and compassion, of indignation against his sins, and pity for his person. It is
possible to feel this deep abhorrence of sin mingled with
deep compassion for souls capable of such endless happiness, and yet bound to eternal misery.

I will explain myself. There are two kinds of love :
one is the love of benevolence. This has no respect to the
character of the person loved, but merely views the individual as exposed to suffering and misery. This God feels
towards all men. The other kind includes esteem or approbation of character. God feels this only towards the
righteous. He never feels *this* love towards sinners. He
infinitely abhors them. He has an infinitely strong exercise of compassion and abhorrence at the same time.
Christians have the same feelings, only not in the same
degree, but they have them at the same time. Probably
they never feel right unless they have both these feelings
in exercise at the same time. The Christian does not feel
as God feels towards individuals nor feel according to the
true character of the individuals, unless both these feelings
exist in his mind at the same time. You see this by one
striking characteristic. The Christian will rebuke most
pointedly and frequently those for whom he feels the deep-
est compassion. Did you never see this ? Did you never

see a parent yearning with compassion over a child, and reprove him with tears, and yet with a pungency that would make the little offender quail under his rebuke. Jesus Christ often manifested strongly these two emotions. He wept over Jerusalem, and yet he tells the reason in a manner that shows his burning indignation against their conduct. " O Jerusalem, thou that killest the prophets and stonest them that are sent unto thee !" Ah, what a full view he had of their wickedness, at the moment that he wept with compassion for the doom that hung over them.

It is just so with this class of Christians. You never find one of them addressing a sinner so as merely to make him weep because somebody is weeping for him. But his tender appeals are accompanied with strong rebuke for sin.

I wish you to remember this point—that the true friend of God and man never takes the sinner's part, because he never acts through mere compassion. And at the same time, he is never seen to denounce the sinner, without at the same time manifesting compassion for his soul and a strong desire to save him from death.

5. It is a prominent object with such Christians, in all their intercourse with men, to make them friends of God.

Whether they converse, or pray, or attend to the duties of life, it is their prominent object to recommend religion and to lead every body to glorify God. It is very natural they should do this, if they are true friends of God. A true friend of the government wishes everybody to be a friend of the government. A true and affectionate child wishes everybody to love and respect his father. And if any one is at enmity, it is his constant aim and effort to bring him to reconciliation. The same you would expect from a true friend of God, as a leading feature of his character, that he would make it a *prominent* object of his life to reconcile sinners to God.

Now mark me ! If this is not the leading feature of

your character, if it is not the absorbing topic of thought
and effort to reconcile men to God, you have not the root
of the matter in you.   Whatever appearance of religion
you may have, you lack the leading and fundamental characteristic of true piety.   It wants the leading feature of
the character and aims of Jesus Christ, and of his apostles
and prophets.   Look at them, and see how this feature
stands out in strong and eternal relief, as the leading characteristic, the prominent design and object, of their lives.
Now let me ask you, what is the leading object of your
life, as it appears in your daily walk ?   Is it to bring all
God's enemies to submit to him ?   If not, away with your
pretensions to religion.   Whatever else you may have, you
have not the true love of God in you.

6. Where there are persons of this class, you will see
them scrupulously avoid everything that in their estimation
is calculated to defeat their great end.

They always wish to avoid every thing calculated to
prevent the salvation of souls, everything calculated to
divert attention or in any way to hinder the conversion of
souls.   It is not the natural question with them, when
any thing is proposed which is doubtful, to ask, "Is this
something which God expressly forbids ?"   The first question that naturally suggests itself to their minds is, "What
will be the bearing of this upon religion ?   Will it have a
tendency to prevent the conversion of sinners, to hinder the
progress of revivals, to roll back the wheels of salvation ?"
If so, they do not need the thunders of Sinai to be pealed
in their ears, to forbid their doing it.   If they see it contrary to the spirit of holiness, and contrary to the main
object they have in view, that is enough.

Look at the temperance reformation for an illustration
of this.   Here let me say, that it was the influence of intemperance, in hindering the conversion and salvation of
sinners, that first turned the attention of the benevolent

men who commenced the reformation, to inquire on the subject. And the same class of persons are still carrying it on. Such men do not stand and cavil at every step of the way, and say, " Drinking rum is no where prohibited in the Bible, and I do not feel bound to give it up." They find that it hinders the great object for which they live, and that is enough for them—they give it up of course. They avoid whatever they see would hinder a revival, as a matter of course, just as a merchant would avoid anything that had a tendency to impair his credit, and defeat his object of making money by his business. Suppose a merchant was about to do something that you knew would injuriously affect his credit, and you go to him in the spirit of friendship and advise him not to do it, would he turn round and say, " Show me the passage in the Bible where God has prohibited this ?" No. He would not ask you to show him anything more than this, that it is inconsistent with his main design.

Mark this, all of you : A person who is strongly desirous of the conversion of sinners does not need an express prohibition to prevent his doing that which he sees is calculated to prevent this. There is no danger of his doing that which will defeat the very object of his life.

7. This class of professing Christians are always distressed unless they see the work of converting sinners going on.

They call it a lamentable state of things in the church, if no sinners are converted. No matter what else is true, no matter how rich the congregation grows, nor how popular their minister, nor how many come to hear him, their panting hearts are uneasy unless they see the work of conversion actually going on. They see that all the rest is nothing without this—yea, that even the means of grace are doing more hurt than good, unless sinners are converted.

Such professors as these are a great trouble to those who are religious from other motives, and who therefore wish to keep all quiet, and have everything go on regularly in the "good old way." They are often called "uneasy spirits in the church." And mark it! if a church has a few such spirits in it, the minister will be made uneasy unless his preaching is such as to convert sinners. You sometimes hear of these men reproving the church, and pouring out their expostulations for living so coldly and worldly, and the church reply, "O, we are doing well enough, do you not see how we flourish, it is only because you are always uneasy." When in fact their hearts are grieved and their souls in agony because sinners are not converted and souls are pressing down to, hell.

8. You will see them when manifesting a spirit of prayer, praying not for themselves but for sinners.

If you know the habitual tenor of people's prayers, it will show which way the tide of their feelings sets. If a man is actuated in religion mainly by a desire to save himself, you will hear him praying chiefly for himself—that he may have his sins pardoned and "enjoy" much of the Spirit of God, and the like. But if he is truly the friend of God and man, you will find that the burden of his prayers is for the glory of God in the salvation of sinners; and he is never so copious and powerful in prayer as when he gets upon his favorite topic—the conversion of sinners. Go into the prayer meeting where such Christians pray, and instead of seeing them all shut up in the nut shell of their own interests, spending their whole prayer on themselves, and just closing with a flourish about the kingdom of Christ, you will hear them pouring out their souls in prayer for the salvation of sinners. I believe there have been cases of such Christians who were so much absorbed in their desires for the salvation of sinners, that for weeks together they did not even pray for their own salvation.

Or if they pray for themselves at all, it is that they may be clothed with the Spirit of God, so that they can go out and be mighty through God in pulling souls out of the fire.

You that are here can tell how it is with your prayers, whether you feel most and pray most for yourselves or for sinners. If you know nothing about the spirit of prayer for sinners, you are not the true friend of God and man. What! no heart to feel when sinners are going to hell by your side! No sympathy with the Son of God, who gave his life to save sinners! Away with all such professions of religion. "If any man have not the Spirit of Christ, he is none of His." Do not tell me men are truly pious, when their prayers are droned over, as much a matter of form as when the poor popish priest counts over his beads. Such a man deceives himself, if he talk about being the true friend of God and man.

9. These persons do not want to ask what are the things they are "required" to do for the conversion of sinners.

When anything is presented to them that promises success in converting sinners, they do not wait to be commanded to do it, on pains and penalties if they do not. They only want the evidence that it is calculated to advance the object on which their hearts are set, and they will engage in it with all their soul. The question is not with them all the while, "What am I expressly commanded to do?" but, "In what way can I do most for the salvation of souls, and the conversion of the world to God?" They do not wait for an express command in the Bible, before they engage in the work of missions, or Sabbath schools, or any other enterprise that promises to save souls; but they are ready to every good word and work.

10. Another characteristic of such Christians is a disposition to deny themselves to do good to others.

God has established throughout all the universe the

principle of GIVING. Even in the natural world, the rivers, the ocean, the clouds, all give. It is so throughout the whole kingdom of nature and of grace. This diffusive principle is every where recognized. This is the very spirit of Christ. He sought not to please himself, but to do good to others. He found his highest happiness in denying himself to do good to others. So it is with this class of persons—they are ever ready to deny themselves of enjoyments and comforts, and even of necessaries, when by so doing they can do more good to others.

11. They are continually devising new means and new measures for doing good.

This is what would be expected from their continual desire to do good. Instead of being satisfied with what does not succeed, they are continually devising new ways and means to effect their object. They are not like those persons who make themselves satisfied with doing what they call their *duty*. Where an individual is aiming mainly at his own salvation, he may think if he does his duty he is discharged from responsibility, and so he is satisfied—he thinks he has escaped from divine wrath and gained heaven for himself, by doing what God required him to do, and he cannot help it, whether sinners are saved or lost. But with the other class, it is not so much their object to gain heaven and avoid wrath, but their leading object is to save souls and to honor God. And if this object is not advanced, they are in pain. Such a man is the one whose soul is all the while devising liberal things, and trying new things, and if one fails, trying another and another, and cannot rest till he has found something that will succeed in the salvation of souls.

12. They always manifest great grief when they see the church asleep and doing nothing for the salvation of sinners.

They know the difficulty—the impossibility of doing

any thing considerable for the salvation of sinners while the church is asleep. Go into a church where the great mass are doing nothing for the conversion of sinners, and floating along on the current of the world, and you will find that the true friends of God and man are grieved at such a state of things. Those who have other objects in view in being religious, may think they are going on very well. They are not grieved when they see the professed people of God going after show and folly. But if there are any of this class, you will find them grieved and distressed at heart, because the church is in such a state.

13. They are grieved if they see reason to think their minister temporizes, or does not reprove the church pointedly and faithfully for their sins.

The other classes of professors are willing to be rocked to sleep, and willing their minister should preach smooth, flowery, and eloquent sermons, and flattering sermons, with no point and no power. But these are not satisfied unless he preaches powerfully and pointedly, and boldly, and rebukes and entreats and exhorts, with all long-suffering and doctrine. Their souls are not fed, or edified, or satisfied with any thing that does not take hold, and do the work for which the ministry was appointed by Jesus Christ.

14. This class of persons will always stand by a faithful minister, who preaches the truth boldly and pointedly.

No matter if the truth he preaches hits them, they like it, and say, Let the righteous smite me, and it shall be an excellent oil. When the truth is poured forth with power, their souls are fed, and grow strong in grace. They can pray for such a minister. They can weep in their closet, and pour out their souls in prayer for him, that he may have the Spirit of God always with him. While others scold and cavil at him and talk about his being extravagant, and all that, you will find Christians of this sort will stand

by him, yea, and would go to the stake with him for the
testimony of Jesus. And this they do for the best of all
reasons—such preaching falls in with the great design for
which these Christians live.

15. This sort of Christians are especially distressed
when ministers preach sermons not adapted to convert
sinners.

I mean when the sermon is not especially addressed to
the church, to stir them up.   Others may approve the
sermon, and praise it, and tell what a great sermon it is,
or how eloquent, or lucid, or grand, or sublime, but it
does not suit THEM if it lacks this one characteristic—a
tendency to convert sinners. You will find some people
that are great sticklers for the doctrine of election, and
they will not believe it is a gospel sermon unless it has the
doctrine of election in it, but if the doctrine of election is
in it they are suited whether it is adapted to convert sinners or not. But where a man has his heart set on the
conversion of sinners, if he hears a sermon not calculated
to do this, he feels as if it lacked the "great thing" that
constitutes a gospel sermon. But if they hear a sermon
calculated to save souls, then they are fed, and their souls
rejoice.

Hence you see the ground for the astonishing difference
you often find in the judgment which people pass upon
preaching. There is in fact no better test of character
than this. It is easy to see who they are that are filled
with the love of God and of souls, by the judgment which
they pass upon preaching. The true friends of God and
man, when they hear a sermon that is not particulary designed to probe and rouse the church and bring them to
action, if it is not such as to bear down on sinners and
does not tend to convert sinners, it is not the sermon for
them.

16. You will always find this class of persons speaking

in terms of dissatisfaction with themselves, that they do no more for the conversion of sinners.

However much they may really " do" for this object, it seems that the more they do the more they long to do. They are never satisfied. Instead of being satisfied with the present degree of their success, there is no end of their longing for the conversion of sinners. I recollect a good man, who used to pray till he was exhausted with praying for individuals, and for places, and for the world's conversion. Once when he was quite exhausted with praying, he exclaimed " Oh ! my longing, aching heart ! There is no such thing as satisfying my unutterable desires for the conversion of sinners. My soul breaketh for the longing that it hath." That man, though he had been useful beyond almost any other man of his age, yet he saw so much to do, and he so longed to see the work go forward and sinners saved, that his mortal frame could not sustain it. " I find," said he, one day, " that I am dying for want of strength to do more to save the souls of men. Oh, how much I want strength, that I may save souls."

17. If you wish to move this class of persons, you must make use of motives drawn from their great and leading object.

If you wish to move them, you must hold up the situation of sinners, and show how they dishonor God, and you will find this will move their souls and set them on fire sooner than any appeal to their hopes and fears. Roll on them this great object. Show them how they can convert sinners, and their longing hearts beat and wrestle with God in prayer, and travail for souls, until they see them converted, and Christ formed in them the hope of glory.

I might mention many other characteristics which belong to this class of professing Christians—the true friends of God and man, did time and strength permit. But I must stop here, and postpone the consideration of the other two classes till next Friday evening, if we are spared, and the Lord permit.

Now, do you belong to this class, or not ? I have mentioned certain great fundamental facts, which, when they exist, indicate the true character of individuals, by showing what is their main design and object in life. You can tell whether this is your character. When I come to the other part of the subject, I shall endeavor to describe those classes of professing Christians, whose religious zeal, prayers, and efforts, have another design, and show their character, and how this design is carried out.

And now, beloved, I asked you before God, have you these characteristics of a child of God ? Do you *know* they belong to you ? Can you say, " O Lord, thou knowest all things, thou knowest that I love thee, and that these are the features of my character !"

5

LEGAL RELIGION

"Who is on the Lord's side?"   Exodus 32:26.

LAST Friday evening, you will remember, that in discoursing from this text, I mentioned three classes of professors of religion : those who truly love God and man, those who are actuated solely by selfishness (or at most self-love) in their religious duties, and those who are actuated only by a regard for public opinion.   I also mentioned several characteristics of the first class, by which they may be known.   This evening I intend to mention several characteristics of the second class,

Those professors who are actuated by self-love or by selfishness.

I design to show how their leading or main design in religion develops itself in their conduct.   The conduct of men invariably shows what is their true and main design. A man's character is as his supreme object is.   And if you can learn by his conduct what that leading object is, then you can know with certainty what his character is. And I suppose this may generally be known by us with great certainty, if we would candidly and thoroughly observe their conduct.

These three classes of professors agree in many things, and it would be impossible to discriminate between them by an observation of these things only.   But there are certain things in which they differ, and by close observation the difference will be seen in their conduct, from which we infer a difference in their character.   And those points in which they differ belong to the very fundamental of religion.

75

I will now proceed to mention some of the characteristics of the second class—those who are actuated by self-love, or by selfishness, in whom hope and fear are the main springs of all they do in religion. And the things that I shall mention are such as, when they are seen, make it evident that the individual is actuated by a supreme regard to his own good, and that the fear of evil, or the hope of advantage to himself, is the foundation of all his conduct.

1. They make religion a subordinate concern.

They show by their conduct that they do not regard religion as the principal business of life, but as subordinate to other things. They consider religion as something that ought to come in by the by, as something that ought to come in and find a place among other things, as a sort of Sabbath-day business, or something to be confined to the closet and the hour of family prayer, and the Sabbath, out not as the grand business of life. They make a distinction between religious duty and business, and consider them as entirely separate concerns. Whereas, if they had right views of the matter, they would consider religion as the *only* business of life, and nothing else either lawful or worth pursuing, any further than as it promotes or subserves religion. If they had the right feeling, religion would characterize all that they do, and it would be manifest that everything they do is an act of obedience to God, or an act of irreligion.

2. Their religious duties are performed as a task, and are not the result of the constraining love of God that burns within them.

Such a one does not delight in the exercise of religious affections; and as to communion with God, he knows nothing of it. He performs prayer as a task. He betakes himself to religious duties as sick persons take medicine, not because they love it, but because they hope to derive some benefit from it.

And here let me ask those who are present to-night, Do you enjoy religious exercises, or do you perform them because you hope to receive benefit by them ? Be honest, now, and answer this question, just according to the truth, and see where you stand.

3. They manifestly possess a legal spirit, and not a gospel spirit.

They do rather what they are obliged to do, in religion, and not what they love to do. They have an eye to the commands of God, and yield obedience to his requirements, in performing religious duties, but do not engage in those things because they love them. They are always ready to inquire, in regard to duty, not so much how they can do good, as how they can be saved. There is just the difference between them, that there is between a convinced sinner and a true convert. The convinced sinner asks, " What must I do to be saved ? " The true convert asks, " Lord, what wilt thou have me to do ? " So this class of professors are constantly asking, " What must I do to get to heaven ? " and not " What can I do to get other people there ? " The principal object of such a professor of religion is not to save the world, but to save himself.

4. They are actuated by fear much more than by hope.

They perform their religious duties chiefly because they dare not omit them. They go to the communion, not because they love to meet Christ, or because they love to commune with their brethren, but because they dare not stay away. They fear the censures of the church, or they are afraid they shall be damned if they neglect it. They perform their closet duties not because they enjoy communion with God, but because they dare not neglect them. They have the spirit of slaves, and go about the service of God, as slaves go about the service of their master, feeling that they are obliged to do about so much, or be beaten with many stripes. So these professors feel as if they were obliged to have about so much religion, and perform about so many religious duties, or be lashed by conscience and lose their hopes. And therefore they go through, painfully and laboriously enough, with about so many religious duties in a year, and that they call religion !

5. Their religion is not only produced by the fear of disgrace or the fear of hell, but it is mostly of a negative character.

They satisfy themselves, mostly, with doing nothing that is very bad. Having no spiritual views, they regard the law of God chiefly as a system of prohibitions, just to guard men from certain sins, and not as a system of benevolence fulfilled by love. And so, if they are moral in their conduct, and tolerably serious and decent in their general deportment, and perform the required amount of religious exercises, this satisfies them. Their conscience harasses them, not so much about sins of omission as sins of commission. They make a distinction between neglecting to do what God positively requires, and doing what he positively forbids. The most you can say of them is, that they are not very bad. They seem to think little or nothing of being useful to the cause of Christ, so long as they cannot be convicted of any positive transgression.

6. This class of persons are more or less strict in religious duties, according to the light they have and the sharpness with which conscience pursues them.

Where they have enlightened minds and tender consciences, you often find them the most rigid of all professors. They tithe even to mint and annise. They are stiff even to moroseness. They are perfect pharisees, and carry everything to the greatest extremes, so far as outward strictness is concerned.

7. They are more or less miserable in proportion to the tenderness of their conscience.

With all their strictness, they cannot be sensible that

they are great sinners after all : and having no just sense
of the gospel justification, this leaves them very unhappy.
And the more enlightened and tender their conscience, the
more they are unhappy. Notwithstanding their strictness,
they feel that they come short of their duty, and not having any gospel faith, nor any of that holy anointing of the
Holy Spirit that brings peace to the soul, they are unsatisfied, and uneasy, and miserable.

Perhaps many of you have seen such persons. Per-
haps some of you are such, and you never knew what it was
to feel justified before God, through the blood of Jesus
Christ, and you know not what it is to feel that Jesus
Christ has accepted and owned you as his. You never felt
in your minds what that is which is spoken of in the text,
" There is now no condemnation to them that are in Christ
Jesus, who walk not after the flesh, but after the Spirit."
Does such language bring home any warm and practical
idea to you, that it is a reality because you experience it in
your soul ? Or do you, after all, still feel condemned and
guilty, and have no sense of pardoned sin, and no experi-
mental peace with God, or confidence in Jesus Christ.

8. This class of persons are encouraged and cheered by
reading the accounts of ancient saints who fell into great
sins.

They feel wonderfully instructed and edified when they
hear the sins of God's people set forth in a strong light.
Then they are comforted and their hopes are wonderfully
strengthened. Instead of feeling humbled and distressed,
and feeling that such conduct is so contrary to all religion
that they could hardly believe they were saints if it had
not been found in the Bible, and that they could not believe at all that persons who should do such things under
the light of the Christian dispensation, could be saints ;
they feel gratified and strengthened, and their hopes con-
firmed, by all these things. I once knew a man, an elder

too, brought before the session of a church for the crime
of adultery, and he actually excused himself by this plea :
He did not know, he said, why he should be expected to
be better than David, the man after God's own heart.

9. They are always much better pleased, by how much
the lower the standard of piety is held out from the pulpit.

If the minister adopts a low standard, and is ready
charitably to hope that almost every body is a Christian,
they are pleased, and compliment him for his expansive
charity, and praise him as such an excellent man, so charitable, etc.   It is easy to see why this class of persons are
pleased with such an exhibition of Christianity.   It subserves their main design.   It helps them to maintain what
they call a " comfortable hope," notwithstanding they do
so little for God.   Right over against this, you will see, is
the conduct of the man whose main design is to rid the
world of *sin*.   He wants all men to be holy, and therefore he wants to have the true standard of holiness held up.
He wants all men to be saved, but he knows they cannot
be saved unless they are truly holy.   And he would as soon
think of Satan's going to heaven as of getting a man there
by frittering away the Bible standard of holiness by
" charity."

10. They are fond of having " comfortable " doctrines
preached.

Such persons are apt to be fond of having the doctrine
of saints' perseverance much dwelt on, and the doctrine of
election.   Often, they want nothing else but what they
call the doctrines of grace.   And if they can be preached
in such an abstract way, as to afford them comfort without galling their consciences too much, they are fed.

11. They love to have their ministers preach sermons
" to feed Christians."

Their main object is not to save sinners, but to be saved
themselves, and therefore they always choose a minister,

not for his ability in preaching for the conversion of sinners, but for his talents in feeding the church with mere abstractions.

12. They lay great stress on having "a comfortable hope."

You will hear them talking very solemnly about the importance of having a comfortable hope. If they can only enjoy their minds, they show very little solicitude whether anybody else around them is saved or not. If they can have only their fears silenced and their hopes cherished they have religion enough to satisfy them.

Right over against this, you will find the true friends of God and man are thinking mainly of something else : they are trying to pull sinners out of the fire, and do not spend their energy in sustaining a comfortable hope for themselves.

In their prayers, you will find the class I am now speaking of, are praying mainly that their evidences may be brightened, and that they may feel assured that they are going to heaven, and know that they are accepted of God. Their great object is to secure their hopes, and so they pray that their evidences may be brightened, instead of praying that their faith may be strengthened, and their souls full of the Holy Ghost to pull sinners out of the fire.

13. They live very much on their own frames of mind.

They lay great stress on the particular emotions which they have from time to time. If at any time they have some high-wrought feelings of a religious nature, they dwell on them, and make this evidence last a great while. One such season of excitement will prop up their hopes as long as they can distinctly call it up to remembrance. No matter if they are not doing anything NOW, and are conscious they have no exercises of love to God now, they recollect the time when they had such and such feelings, and that answers to keep alive their hopes. If there has been a revival, and they mingled in its scenes until their imagination has been wrought up so that they could weep and pray and exhort with feeling during a revival, that will last them a long time, and they will have a comfortable hope for years on the strength of it. Although, after the revival is over, they do nothing to promote religion, and their hearts are as hard as adamant, they have a very comfortable hope all the while, patiently waiting for a revival to come and give them another move.

Are any of you who are here now, propping yourselves up by your past frames and feelings, leaning on evidences, not from what you are NOW doing but something that you felt last year, or years ago ? Let me tell you, that if you are thus living on past experience, you will find it will fail when you come to need it.

14. They pray almost exclusively for themselves.

If you could listen at the door of their closets, you would hear eight-tenths of all their petitions going up for themselves. It shows how they value their own salvation in comparison with the salvation of others. It is as eight to two. And if they pray in meetings, very often it will be just the same, and you would not suppose, from their prayers, that they knew there was a sinner on earth travelling the road to hell. They pray for themselves just as they do in the closet, only they couple the rest of the church with them so as to say " we."

15. Such persons pray to be fitted for death much more than they pray to be fitted to live a useful life.

They are more anxious to be prepared to die, than to be prepared to save sinners around them. If they ask for the Spirit of God, they want it to prepare them to die, more than as the Psalmist prayed, " Then will I teach transgressors thy ways, and sinners shall be converted unto thee." How many of you are of this character ? How many are there here, whose prayers are described exactly ?

An individual who made it his great absorbing object to
do good and save sinners, would not be apt to think so
much about when, or where, or how he shall die, as how
he may do the most good while he lives. And as to his
death, he leaves that all to God, and he is not afraid to
leave it all with him. He has long ago given his soul up
to him, and now the great question with him is not, When
shall I die ? but, How shall I live so as to honor God ?

16. They are more afraid of punishment than they are
of sin.

Precisely over against this, you will find the true friends
of God and man more afraid of sin than of punishment.
It is not the question with them, " If I do this shall I be
punished ? " or, " If I do this, will God forgive me ? " But
the question is that which Joseph asked, " How can I do
this great wickedness, and sin against God ? " There was
the spirit of a child of God, afraid of sin more than punishment, and so much afraid of sin that he had no thought
of punishment.

This class of persons I am speaking of, often indulge
in sin if they can persuade themselves that God will forgive them, or when they think they can repent of it afterwards. They often reason in this way : " Such a minister
does this ; " or " Such an elder or professor does this, and
why may not I do the same ? " There was a member of
this church had a class in the Sabbath school ; but seeing
that others did not take a class, the individual reasoned in
this way : " Why should I do it any more than they ? "
and so gave up the class. Here is the spirit of this whole
description of professors—" Others get along without doing such and such things, and why should I trouble myself to be better than they ? " It is not sin that they
fear, but punishment. They sin, *they know*, but they
hope to escape punishment. Who cannot see that this is
contrary to the spirit of the true friends of God, whose

absorbing object it is to get sin, and all sin, out of the world ? Such persons are not half so much afraid of hell as they are of committing sin.

17. They feel and manifest greater anxiety about being saved themselves, than if all the world was going to hell.

Such a professor, if his hope begins to fail, wants to have everybody engaged, to pray for HIM, and make a great ado, and move all the church, when he never thinks of doing anything for the sinners around him, who are certainly on the road to hell. He shows that his mind is absorbed in himself, and that his main design is not to see how much good he can do.

18. They are more fond of receiving good than of doing good.

You may know such persons have not the spirit of the gospel. They have never entered into the spirit of Jesus Christ, when he said, "It is more blessed to give than to receive." A person actuated by true love to God and man, enjoys what he does to benefit others, far more than they do who receive good at his hand. He is really benevolent, and it is a gratification to him to show kindness, because his heart is set upon it, and when he can do it, a holy joy is shed over his mind, and he enjoys it exquisitely.

The other class are more eager to receive than to impart. They want to receive instruction more than to impart it. They want to receive comfort, but are never ready to deny themselves to give the comforts of the gospel to others. How directly contrary this is to the diffusive spirit of the gospel, any one can see at a glance. *That* spirit finds its supreme happiness in communicating happiness to others. But this class of persons want to lay everybody under contribution to impart happiness to themselves, instead of laying themselves out to bless others.

Who does not know these two classes of professors ?— One always seeking out objects to do good to, the other always trying to gain good themselves. One anxious to communicate, the other to receive. One to do good, the other to get good. These two classes of character are just as opposite as light and darkness.

19. If this class of professors are led to pray for the conversion and salvation of others, you may observe that they are actuated by the same kind of considerations as they are when they pray for themselves.

They are chiefly afraid of hell themselves, and when they are strongly convicted, they are afraid others will go there too. They are seeking happiness for themselves, and when self is not in the way, they seek the same for others. They pray for sinners, not because they have such a sense of the evil of sin which sinners are committing, as because they have such a sense of the terrors of hell to which sinners are going. It is not because sinners dishonor God that they want them converted, but because they are in danger. Their great object in praying is to secure the safety of those they pray for, as it is their great object in religion to secure their own safety. They pity themselves and they pity others. If there was no danger, they would have no motive to pray either for themselves or others.

The true friends of God and man feel compassion for sinners too, but they feel much more for the honor of God. They are more distressed to see God abused and dishonored than to see sinners go to hell. And if God must be for ever dishonored or men go to hell—just as certainly as they love God supremely, they will decide that sinners shall sink to endless torments sooner than God fail of his due honor. And they manifest their true feelings in their prayers. You hear them praying for sinners as rebels against God, as guilty criminals deserving of eternal wrath, as the enemies of God and the universe ; and while they are full of compassion for sinners, they feel also the enkindlings of holy indignation against them for their conduct towards the blessed God.

20. The class of professors I am speaking of are very apt to be distressed with doubts.

They are apt to talk a great deal about their doubts. This makes up a great part of their history—the detail of their doubts. The great thing with them being the enjoyment of a comfortable hope, as soon as they begin to doubt, it is all over with them, and so they make a great ado with their doubts, and then they are not prepared to do anything for religion because they have these doubts. The true friends of God and man being engaged in doing good, if the devil at any time suggests that they are going to hell, the first answer they think of is, " What if I should ? Only let me pull sinners out of the fire while I can." I suppose real Christians may have doubts. But they are much less apt to have them, by how much the more they are fully bent on saving sinners. It will be very hard work for Satan to get a church who is fully engaged in the work to be much troubled with doubts. Their attention is not on that, but on something else, and he cannot get the advantage over them.

21. They manifest great uneasiness at the increasing calls for self-denial to do good.

Said an individual, " What will this temperance reformation come to ? At first they only went against ardent spirit, and I gave up that, and did very well without it. Then they called on us to give up wine ; and now they are calling on us to give up our tea and coffee, and tobacco ;— where will it end ? " This class of persons are in constant distress at being called on to give up so much. The good that is to be done does not enter into their thoughts, because they are all the while dwelling on what they have to give up.

It is easily seen why it is that these aggressive movements on the kingdom of darkness distress such persons. Their object never was to search out and banish from this world everything that is dishonorable to God or injurious to man. They never entered upon religion with the determination to clear out every such thing from the earth, as far as they had power, and as fast as they were convinced that it was injurious to themselves or others, in soul or body. And therefore they are distressed by the movements of those who are truly engaged to search out and clear away every evil.

These persons are annoyed by the continually increasing calls to give for missions, Bibles, tracts, and the like. The time was, when a rich man gave twenty-five dollars a year to such things, he was thought to be doing pretty well. But now there are so many calls for subscriptions and contributions, that they are in torment all the time. "I don't like these contributions, I am opposed to having contributions taken up in the congregation, I think they do hurt." They feel specially sore at these agents. "I don't know about these beggars that are going about." They are obliged to keep giving all the time, in order to keep up their character, or to have any hope, but they are much distressed about it, and do not know what the world is coming to, things are in such a strange pass.

As you raise the general standard of living in the church, this class of professors find they have to come up too, lest their hopes should be shaken. And the common standard of professors has been raised already so much, that I have no doubt it costs this class of persons now four times as much of what they call religion, to keep up a hope, as it did twenty years ago. And what will become of them if there are to be so many new movements and new measures, and so much done to save the world? The Lord help them, for they are in great distress!

22. When they are called upon to exercise self-denial

for the sake of doing good, instead of being a pleasant thing, it gives them unmingled pain.

Such a one does not know anything about enjoying self-denial. He cannot understand how self-denial is pleasant, nor how anybody can take pleasure in it, or have joy of heart in denying himself for the sake of doing good to others. That, he thinks, is a height in religion to which he has not attained. Yet the true friend of God and man, whose heart is fully set to do good, never enjoys any money he expends so well as that which he gives to promote Christ's kingdom. If he is really pious, he knows that is the best disposition he can make of his money. Nay, he is sorry to be obliged to use money for anything else, when there are so many opportunities to do good with it.

I want you who are here to look at this. It is easy to see that if an individual has his heart very much set upon anything, all the money he can save for that object is most pleasing to him, and the more he can save from other objects for this that his heart is set on, the better he is pleased. If an individual find it hard for him to give money for religious objects, it is easy to see that his heart is not set on it. If it were, he would have given his money with joy. What would you think of a man who should set himself against giving money for the advancement of religion, and get up an excitement in the church, about the missionary cause, and having so many calls for money, when he had never given five dollars? It would be absolute demonstration that his heart was not truly set on the cause of Christ; if it were, he would give his money for it, as free as water; and the more he could spare for it, the better he would be pleased.

23. This class of persons are not forward in promoting revivals.

This is not their great object. They always have to be dragged into the work. When a revival has begun, and gone on, and the excitement is great, then they come in and appear to be engaged in it. But you never see them taking the lead, or striking out a-head of the rest, and saying to the rest of the brethren, Come on and let us do something for the Lord.

24. As a matter of fact, they do not convert sinners to God.

They may be instrumental of good, in various ways, and so may Satan be instrumental of good. But as a general thing, they do not pull sinners out of the fire. And the reason is, that this is not their great object. How is it with you ? Do you absolutely succeed in converting sinners ? Is there any one who will look to you as the instrument of his conversion ? If you were truly engaged for this, you could not rest satisfied without doing it, and you would go about it so much in earnest, and with such agonizing prayer that you would do it.

25. They do not manifest much distress when they behold sin.

They do not rebuke it. They love to mingle in scenes where sin is committed. They love to be where they can hear vain conversation, and even to join in it. They love worldly company and worldly books. Their spirit is worldly. Instead of hating even the garment spotted with the flesh, they love to hang around the confines of sin, as if they had complacency in it.

26. They take but very little interest in published accounts of revivals, missions, etc.

If any of the missions are tried severely, they neither know nor feel it. If missions prosper, they never know it they take no interest in it. Very likely they do not take any religious paper whatever. Or if they do, when they sit down to read it, if they come to a revival, they pass it over, to read the secular news, or the controversy, or something else. The other class, the true friends of God and man, on the contrary, love to learn the progress of revivals. They love to read a religious paper, and when they take it up, the first thing they do is to run their eye over it to find where there are revivals, and there they feast their souls, and give glory to God. And so with missions: their heart goes forth with the missionaries, and when they hear that the Lord has poured forth his Spirit on a mission, they feel a glow of holy joy thrill through them.

27. They do not aim at any thing higher than a legal, painful, negative religion.

The love of Christ does not constrain them to a constant warfare against sin, and a constant watch to do all the good in their power. But what they do is done only because they think they must. And they maintain a kind of piety that is formal, heartless, worthless.

28. They come reluctantly into all the special movements of the church for doing good.

If a protracted meeting is proposed, you will generally find this class of persons hanging back, and making objections, and raising difficulties as long as they can. If any other special effort is proposed, they come reluctantly, and prefer the good old way. They feel sore at being obliged to add so much every year to their religion in order to maintain their hope.

29. They do not enjoy secret prayer.

They do not pray in their closets because they LOVE to pray but because they think it is their duty, and they dare not neglect it.

30. They do not enjoy the Bible.

They do not read the Bible because it is sweet to their souls, sweeter than honey or the honey-comb. They do not " enjoy " the reading, as a person enjoys the most exquisite delights. They read it because it is their duty to read it ; and it would not do to profess to be a Christian and not read the Bible : but in fact they find it a dry book.

31. They do not enjoy prayer meetings.

Slight excuses keep them away. They never go unless they find it necessary for the sake of keeping up appearances, or to maintain their hope. And when they do go, instead of having their souls melted and fired with love, they are cold, listless, dull, and glad when it is over.

32. They are very much put to it to understand what is meant by disinterestedness.

To serve God because they love him, and not for the sake of the reward, is what they do not understand.

33. Their thoughts are not anxiously fixed upon the question, When shall the world be converted to God ?

Their hearts are not agonized with such thoughts as this, Oh, how long shall wickedness prevail ? Oh, when shall this wretched world be rid of sin and death ? Oh, when shall men cease to sin against God ? They think much more of the question, When shall I die and go to heaven, and get rid of all my trials and cares ?

But I find I am again obliged to omit the examination of the last class of professors till next Friday evening, when, with the leave of Providence, it will be attended to.

CONCLUSION

1. I believe you will not think me extravagant, when I say that the religion I have described, appears to be the religion of a very large mass in the church.

To say the least, it is greatly to be feared that a majority of professing Christians are of this description. To say this, is neither uncharitable nor censorious.

2. This religion is radically defective.

There is nothing of true Christianity in it. It differs from Christianity as much as the Pharisees differed from Christ—as much as gospel religion differs from legal religion.

Now, let me ask you, to which of these classes do you

belong ?   Or are you in neither ?   It may be that because
you are conscious you do not belong to the second class,
you may think you belong to the first, when in fact, you
will find, when I come to describe the third class of professors, that I describe your true character.

How important it is that you know for a certainty what
is your true character—whether you are actuated in religion by true love to God and man, or whether you are
religious only out of regard to yourself.   O, what a solemn
thought, if this church, of which I have been the pastor,
have never come to an intelligent decision of the question,
whether they are the true friends of God and man or not.
Do settle it, beloved.   Now is the time.   Settle this, and
then go to work for God.

6

CONFORMITY TO THE WORLD

"Be not conformed to this world." Romans 12:2.

IT will be recollected by some who are present, that some time since I made use of this text in preaching in this place, but the object of this evening's discourse is so far different that it is not improper to employ the same text again. The following is the order in which I design to discuss the subject of

CONFORMITY TO THE WORLD.

I. To show what is NOT meant by the command of the text.

II. Show what is meant by the command, "Be not conformed to this world."

III. To mention some of the reasons why this requirement is made upon all who will live a godly life.

IV. To answer some objections that are made to the principles laid down.

I. I am to show what is not meant by the requirement, "Be not conformed to this world."

I suppose it is not meant, that Christians should refuse to benefit by the useful arts, improvements, and discoveries of the world. It is not only the privilege but the duty of the friends of God to avail themselves of these, and to use for God all the really useful arts and improvements that arise among mankind.

II. I am to show what is meant by the requirement.

It is meant that Christians are bound not to conform to the world in the three following things. I mention only these three, not because there are not many other things in which conformity to the world is forbidden, but because these three classes are all that I have had time to examine to-night, and further, because these three are peculiarly necessary to be discussed at the present time. The three things are three departments of life, in which it is required that you be not conformed to this world. They are

BUSINESS, FASHION, POLITICS.

In all these departments it is required that Christians should not do as the world do, they should neither receive the maxims, nor adopt the principles, nor follow the practices of the world.

III. I am to mention some reasons for the command, " Be not conformed to this world."

You are by no means to act on the same principles, nor from the same motives, nor pursue your object in the same manner that the world do, either in the pursuits of business, or of fashion, or of politics. I shall examine these several departments separate.

FIRST—*Of Business.*

1. The first reason why we are not to be conformed to this world in business, is, that the principle of the world is that of supreme selfishness. This is true universally, in the pursuit of business. The whole course of business in the world is governed and regulated by the maxims of supreme and unmixed selfishness. It is regulated without the least regard to the commands of God, or the glory of God, or the welfare of their fellow men. The maxims of business generally current among business men, and the habits and usages of business men, are all based upon supreme selfishness. Who does not know, that in making bargains, the business men of the world consult their own interest, and seek their own benefit, and not the benefit of those they deal with ? Who has ever heard of a worldly man of business making bargains, and doing business for

the benefit of those he dealt with ? No, it is always for their own benefit. And are Christians to do so ? They are required to act on the very opposite principle to this : " Let no man seek his own, but every man another's wealth." They are required to copy the example of Jesus Christ. Did he ever make bargains for his own advantage ? And may his followers adopt the principle of the world—a principle that contains in it the seeds of hell ! If Christians are to do this, is it not the most visionary thing on earth to suppose the world is ever going to be converted to the gospel.

2. They are required not to conform to the world, because conformity to the world is totally inconsistent with the love of God or man.

The whole system recognizes only the love of self. Go through all the ranks of business men, from the man that sells candy on the sidewalk at the corner of the street, to the greatest wholesale merchant or importer in the United States, and you will find that one maxim runs through the whole, to " buy as cheap as you can, and sell as dear as you can, to look out for number one," and to do always, as far as the rules of honesty will allow, all that will advance your own interests, let what will become of the interest of others. Ungodly men will not deny that these are the maxims on which business is done in the world. The man who pursues this course is universally regarded as doing business on business principles. Now, are these maxims consistent with holiness, with the love of God or the love of man, with the spirit of the gospel or the example of Jesus Christ ? Can a man conform to the world in these principles, and yet love God ? Impossible ! No two things can be more unlike. Then Christians are by no means to conform to the business maxims of the world.

3. These maxims, and the rules by which business is done in the world, are directly opposite to the gospel of

Jesus Christ and the spirit he exhibited, and the maxims
he inculcated, and the rules which he enjoined that all his
followers should obey, on pain of hell.

What was the spirit Jesus Christ exemplified on earth ?
It was the spirit of self-denial, of benevolence, of sacrific-
ing himself to do good to others.   He exhibited the same
spirit that God does, who enjoys his infinite happiness in
going out of himself to gratify his benevolent heart in doing good to others.   This is the religion of the gospel, to
be like God, not only doing good, but enjoying it, joyfully
going out of self to do good.   This is the gospel maxim :
" it is more blessed to give than to receive."   And again,
" Look not every man on his own things, but every man
also on the things of others."   What says the business
man of the world ?   " Look out for number one."   These
very maxims were made by men who knew and cared no
more for the gospel, than the heathen do.   Why should
Christians conform to such maxims as these ?

4. To conform to the world in the pursuits of business
is a flat contradiction of the engagements that Christians
make when they enter the church.

What is the engagement that you make when you enter
the church ?   Is it not, to renounce the world and live for
God, and to be actuated by the Spirit of Jesus Christ, and
to possess supreme love to God, and to renounce self, and
to give yourself to glorify God, and do good to men ?
You profess not to love the world, its honors, or its riches.
Around the communion table, with your hand on the
broken body of your Saviour, you avouch these to be your
principles, and pledge yourself to live by these maxims.
And then what do you do ?   Go away, and follow maxims
and rules gotten up by men, whose avowed principle is the
love of the world, and whose avowed object is to get the
world ?   Is this your way ?   Then, unless you repent, let
me tell you, you will be damned.   It is no more certain,

that any infidel, or any profligate wretch, will go to hell, than that all such professing Christians will go there, who conform to the world. They have double guilt. They are sworn before God to a different course, and when they pursue the business principles of the world, they show that they are perjured wretches.

5. Conformity to the world is such a manifest contra-diction of the principles of the gospel, that sinners when they see it, do not and cannot understand from it the true nature and object of the gospel itself.

How can they understand that the object of the gos-pel is to raise men above the love of the world, and above the influence of the world, and place them on higher ground, to live on totally different principles? When they see professing Christians acting on the same princi-ples with other men, how can they understand the true principles of the gospel, or know what it means by heavenly-mindedness, self-denial, benevolence, and so on?

6. It is this spirit of conformity to the world, that has already eaten out the love of God from the church.

Show me a young convert, while his heart is warm, and the love of God glows out from his lips. What does he care for the world? Call up his attention to it, point him to its riches, its pleasures, or its honors, and try to engage him in their pursuit, and he loathes the thought. But let him now go into business, and do business on the principles of the world one year, and you no longer find the love of God glowing in his heart, and his religion has become the religion of conscience, dry, meagre, uninflu-ential—anything but the glowing love of God, moving him to acts of benevolence. I appeal to every man in this house, and if my voice was loud enough I would appeal to every professor of religion in this city, if it is not. And if any one should say, "No, it is not so," I should regard it as proof that he *never* knew what it was to feel the glow of a convert's first love.

7. This conformity to the world in business is one of the greatest stumbling-blocks in the way of the conversion of sinners.

What do wicked men think, when they see professing Christians, with such professions on their lips, and pretending to believe what the Bible teaches, and yet driving after the world, as eager as anybody, making the best bargains, and dealing as hard as the most worldly? What do they think? I can tell you what they say. They say, " I do not see but these Christians do just as the rest of us do, they act on the same principles, look out as sharp for number one, drive as hard bargains, and get as high interest as anybody." And it must be said that these are not things of which the world accuse Christians slanderously. It is a notorious fact that most of the members of the church pursue the world, as far as appears, in the same spirit, by the same maxims, and to the same degree, that the ungodly do who maintain a character for uprightness and humanity. The world say, "Look at the church, I don't see as they are any better than I am ; they go to the full length that I do after the world." If professing Christians act on the same principles with worldly men, as the Lord liveth, they shall have the same reward. They are set down in God's book of remembrance as black hypocrites, pretending to be the friends of God while they love the world. For whoso loveth the world is the enemy of God. They profess to be governed by principles directly opposite to the world, and if they do the same things with the world, they are hypocrites.

8. Another reason for the requirement, " Be not conformed to this world," is the immense, salutary and instantaneous influence it would have if everybody would do business on the principles of the gospel.

Just turn the tables over, and let Christians do business one year on gospel principles. It would shake the world. It would ring louder than thunder. Let the ungodly see professing Christians, in every bargain, consulting the good of the person they are trading with—seeking not their own wealth, but every man another's wealth—living above the world—setting no value on the world any farther than it can be a means of glorifying God. What do you think would be the effect ? What effect DID it have in Jerusalem, when the whole body of Christians gave up their business, and turned out in a body to pursue the salvation of the world ? They were only a few ignorant fishermen, and a few humble women, but they turned the world upside down. Let the church live so now, and it would cover the world with confusion of face, and overwhelm them with convictions of sin. Only let them see the church living above the world, and doing business on gospel principles, seeking not their own interests but the interests of their fellow men, and infidelity would hide its head. heresy would be driven from church, and this charming, blessed spirit of love, would go over the world like the waves of the sea.

Secondly.—*Of Fashions.*

Why are Christians required not to follow the fashions of the world ?

1. Because it is directly at war with the spirit of the gospel, and is minding earthly things.

What is minding earthly things, if it is not to follow the fashions of the world, that like a tide are continually setting to and fro, and fluctuating in their forms, and keeping the world continually changing ? There are many men of large business in the world, and men of wealth, who think they care nothing for the fashions. They are occupied with something else, and they trust the fashions altogether with their tailor, taking it for granted that he will make all right. But mind, if he should make a garment unfashionable, you would see that they do care about the fashions, and they never would employ that tailor again. Still, at present their thoughts are not much on the fashions. They have a higher object in view. And they think it beneath the dignity of a minister to preach about fashions. They overlook the fact, that with the greater part of mankind fashion is everything. The greater part of the community are not rich, and never expect to be, but they look to the world to enable them to make a "respectable" appearance, and to bring up their families in a "respectable" manner; that is, to "follow the fashions." Nine-tenths of the population never look at any thing higher, than to do as the world does, or to follow the fashions. For this they strain every nerve. And this is what they set their hearts on, and what they live for.

The merchant and the rich man deceives himself, therefore, if he supposes that fashion is a little thing. The great body of the people mind this, their minds are set upon it, the thing which they look for in life is to have their dress, equipage, furniture, and so on, like other people, in the fashion, or "respectable" as they call it.

2. To conform to the world is contrary to their profession.

When people join the church, they profess to give up the spirit that gives rise to the fashions. They profess to renounce the pomps and vanities of the world, to repent of their pride, to follow the meek and lowly Saviour, to live for God. And now, what do they do? You often see professors of religion go to the extreme of the fashion. Nothing will satisfy them that is not in the height of fashion. And a Christian female dress-maker who is conscientiously opposed to the following of fashions, cannot get her bread. She cannot get employment even among professing Christian ladies, unless she follows the fashions in all their countless changes. God knows it is so, and they must give up their business if their conscience will not permit them to follow the changes of fashion.

3. This conformity is a broad and complete approval of the spirit of the world.

What is it that lies at the bottom of all this shifting scenery? What is the cause that produces all this gaudy show and dash, and display? It is the love of applause. And when Christians follow the changes of fashion, they pronounce all this innocent. All this waste of money and time and thought, all this feeding and cherishing of vanity and the love of applause, the church sets her seal to, when she conforms to the world.

4. Nay, further, another reason is, that following the fashions of the world, professing Christians show that they do in fact love the world.

They show it by their conduct, just as the ungodly show it by the same conduct. As they act alike they give evidence that they are actuated by one principle, the love of fashion.

5. When Christian professors do this, they show most clearly that they love the praise of men.

It is evident that they love admiration and flattery, just as sinners do. Is not this inconsistent with Christian principle, to go right into the very things that are set up by the pride and fashion and lust of the ungodly?

6. Conforming to the world in fashion, you show that you do not hold yourself accountable to God for the manner in which you lay out money.

You practically disown your stewardship of the money that is in your possession. By laying out money to gratify your own vanity and lust, you take off the keen edge of that truth, which ought to cut that sinner in two, who is living to himself. It is practically denying that the earth is the Lord's, with the cattle on a thousand hills, and all to be employed for his glory.

7. You show that reputation is your idol.

When the cry comes to your ears on every wind, from the ignorant and the lost of all nations, "Come over and help us, come over and help us," and every week brings some call to send the gospel, to send tracts, and Bibles, and missionaries, to those who are perishing for lack of knowledge, if you choose to expend money in following the fashions, it is demonstration that reputation is your idol. Suppose now, for the sake of argument that it is not prohibited in the word of God, to follow the fashions, and that professing Christians, if they will, may *innocently* follow the fashions : (I deny that it is innocent, but suppose it were,) does not the fact that they do follow them when there are such calls for money, and time, and thought, and labor to save souls, prove conclusively that they do not love God nor the souls of men ?

Take the case of a woman, whose husband is in slavery, and she is trying to raise money enough for his redemption There she is, toiling and saving, rising up early and sitting up late, and eating the bread of carefulness, because her husband, the father of her children, the friend of her youth, is in slavery. Now go to that woman and tell her that it is innocent for her to follow the fashions, and dress, and display like her neighbors—will she do it ? Why not ? She does not desire to do it. She will scarcely buy a pair of shoes for her feet ; she grudges almost the bread she eats—so intent is she on her great object.

Now suppose a person loved God, and the souls of men, and the kingdom of Christ, does he need an express prohibition from God to prevent him from spending his money and his life in following the fashion ? No, indeed, he will rather need a positive injunction to take what is needful for his own comfort and the support of his own life. Take the case of Timothy. Did he need a prohibition to prevent him from indulging in the use of wine ? So far from it, he was so cautious that it required an express injunction from God to make him drink a little as a medicine. Although he was sick, he would not drink it till he had the word of God for it, he saw the evils of it so clearly. Now, show me a man or woman, I care not what their professions are, that follows the fashions of the world, and I will show you what spirit they are of.

Now, do not ask me why Abraham, and David, and Solomon, who were so rich, did not lay out their money in spreading the kingdom of God ? Ah, tell me, did they enjoy the light that professors now enjoy ? Did they even know so much as this, that the world can be converted, as Christians now see clearly that it can ? But suppose it were as allowable in you as it was in Abraham or David to be rich, and to lay out the property you possess in display, and pomp, and fashion ; suppose it were perfectly innocent, who that loves the Lord Jesus Christ would wish to lay out money in fashion when they could lay it out to gratify the *all-absorbing* passion to do good to the souls of men ?

8. By conforming to the world in fashion, you show that you differ not at all from ungodly sinners.

Ungodly sinners say, " I don't see but that these Christian men and women love to follow the fashions as well as I do." Who does not know, that this leads many to infidelity.

9. By following the fashions you are tempting God to give you up to a worldly spirit.

There are many now that have followed the world, and followed the fashions, till God seems to have given them over to the devil for the destruction of the flesh. They have little or no religious feeling, no spirit of prayer, no zeal for the glory of God or the conversion of sinners : the Holy Spirit seems to have withdrawn from them.

10. You tempt the church to follow the fashions.

Where the principal members, the elders and leaders in the church, and their wives and families, are fashionable Christians, they drag the whole church along with them into the train of fashion, and every one apes them as far as they can, down to the lowest servant. Only let a rich Christian lady come out to the house of God in full fashion, and the whole church are set agog to follow as far as they can, and it is a chance if they do not run in debt to do it.

You tempt yourself to pride and folly and a worldly spirit.

Suppose a man that had been intemperate and was reformed, should go and surround himself with wine and brandy and every seductive liquor, keeping the provocatives of appetite always under his eye, and from time to time tasting a little; does he not tempt himself? Now see that woman that has been brought up in the spirit of pride and show, and that has been reformed, and has professed to abandon them all; let her keep these trappings, and continue to follow the fashions, and pride will drag her backwards as sure as she lives. She tempts herself to sin and folly.

12. You are tempting the world.

You are setting the world into a more fierce and hot pursuit of these things. The very things that the world love, and that they are sure to have scruples about their being right, professing Christians fall in with and follow, and thus tempt the world to continue in the pursuit of what will destroy their souls in hell.

13. By following the fashions, you are tempting the devil to tempt you.

When you follow the fashions, you open your heart to him. You keep it for him, empty, swept, and garnished. Every woman that suffers herself to follow the fashions may rely upon it, she is helping Satan to tempt her to pride and sin.

14. You lay a great stumbling block before the greatest part of mankind.

There are a few persons who are pursuing greater objects than fashion. They are engaged in the scramble for political power, or they are eager for literary distinction, or they are striving for wealth. And they do not know that their hearts are set on fashion at all. They are following selfishness on a larger scale. But the great mass of the community are influenced mostly by these fluctuating fashions. To this class of persons it is a great and sore stumbling block, when they see professing Christians just as prompt and as eager to follow the changing of fashion as themselves. They see, and say, "What does their profession amount to, when they follow the fashions as much as anybody?" or "Certainly it is right to follow the fashions, for see the professing Christians do it as much as we."

15. Another reason why professing Christians are required not to be conformed to the world in fashion is, the great influence their disregarding fashion would have on the world.

If professing Christians would show their contempt for these things, and not pretend to follow them, or regard them, how it would shame the world, and convince the world that they were living for another object, for God and for eternity! How irresistible it would be! What an overwhelming testimony in favor of our religion! Even the apparent renunciation of the world, by many orders of monks, has doubtless done more than anything else to put down the opposition to their religion, and give it currency and influence in the world. Now suppose all this was hearty and sincere, and coupled with all that is consistent and lovely in Christian character, and all that is zealous and bold in labors for the conversion of the world from sin to holiness. What an influence it would have ! What thunders it would pour into the ears of the world, to wake them up to follow after God !

Thirdly.—*In Politics.*

I will show why professing Christians are required not to be conformed to the world in politics.

1. Because the politics of the world are perfectly dishonest.

Who does not know this ? Who does not know that it is the proposed policy of every party to cover up the defects of their own candidate, and the good qualities of the opposing candidate ? And is not this dishonest ? Every party holds up its candidate as a piece of perfection, and then aims to ride himself into office by any means, fair or foul. No man can be an honest man, that is committed to a party, to go with them, let them do what they may. And can a christian do it, and keep a conscience void of offence?

2. To conform to the world in politics is to tempt God.

By falling in with the world in politics, Christians are guilty of setting up rulers over them by their own vote, who do not fear nor love God, and who set the law of God at defiance, break the Sabbath, and gamble, and commit adultery, and fight duels, and swear profanely, and leave the laws unexecuted at their pleasure, and that care not for the weal or woe of their country, so long as they can keep their office. I say Christians do this. "For it is plain that where parties are divided, as they are in this country, there are Christians enough to turn the scale in any election. Now let Christians take the ground that they will not vote for a dishonest man, or a Sabbath-breaker, or gambler, or whoremonger, or duelist, for any office, and no party could ever nominate such a character with any hope of success. But on the present system, where men will let the laws go unexecuted, and give full swing to mobs, or lynch-murders, or robbing the mails, or anything else, so they can run in their own candidate who will give them the offices, any man is a dishonest man that will do it, be he professor or non-professor. And can a Christian do this and be blameless ?

3. By engaging with the world in politics, Christians grieve the Spirit of God.

Ask any Christian politician if he ever carried the Spirit of God with him into a political campaign ? Never. I would by no means be understood to say that Christians should refuse to vote, and to exercise their lawful influence in public affairs. But they ought not to follow a party.

4. By following the present course of politics, you are contributing your aid to undermine all government and order in the land.

Who does not know that this great nation now rocks and reels, because the laws are broken and trampled under foot, and the executive power refuses or dare not act ? Either the magistrate does not wish to put down disorder, or he temporizes and lets the devil rule. And so it is in all parts of the country, and all parties. And can a Christian be consistent with his profession, and vote for such men to office ?

5. You lay a stumbling-block in the way of sinners.

What do sinners think, when they see professing Christians acting with them in their political measures, which they themselves know to be dishonest and corrupt ? They say, " We understand what we are about, we are after office, we are determined to carry our party into power, we are pursuing our own interest ; but these Christians profess to live for another and a higher end, and yet here they come, and join with us, as eager for the loaves and fishes as the rest of us." What greater stumbling-block can they have ?

6. You prove to the ungodly that professing Christains are actuated by the same spirit as themselves.

Who can wonder that the world is incredulous as to the reality of religion ? If they do not look for themselves into the scriptures, and there learn what religion is, if they are governed by the rules of evidence from what they see in the lives of professing Christians, they ought to be incredulous. They ought to infer, so far as this evidence goes, that professors of religion do not themselves believe in it. It is the fact. I doubt, myself, whether the great mass of professors believe the Bible.

7. They show, so far as their evidence can go, that there is no change of heart.

What is it ? Is it going to the communion table once in a month or two, and sometimes to prayer meeting ? Is that a change of heart, when they are just as eager in the scramble for office as any others ? The world must be fools to believe in a change of heart on such evidence.

8. Christians ought to cease from conformity to the world in politics, from the influence which such a course would have on the world.

Suppose Christians were to act perfectly conscientious and consistent in this matter, and to say, "We will not vote for any man to office, unless he fears God, and will rule the people in righteousness." Ungodly men would not set men as candidates, who themselves set the laws at defiance. No. Every candidate would be obliged to show that he was prepared to act from higher motives, and that he would lay himself out to make the country prosperous, and to promote virtue, and to put down vice and oppression and disorder, and to do all he can to make the people happy and *holy !* It would shame the dishonest politicians, to show that the love of God and man is the motive that Christians have in view. And a blessed influence would go over the land like a wave.

IV. I am to answer some objections that are made against the principles here advanced.

1. In regard to business.

Objection. " If we do not transact business on the same principles on which ungodly men do it, we cannot compete with them, and all the business of the world will fall into the hands of the ungodly. If we pursue our business for the good of others, if we buy and sell on the principle of not seeking our own wealth, but the wealth of those we do business with, we cannot sustain a competition with worldly men, and they will get all the business."

Let them have it, then. You can support yourself by your industry in some humbler calling, and let worldly men do all the business.

" Objection. " But then, how should we get money to spread the gospel ?"

A holy church that would act on the principles of the gospel, would spread the gospel faster than all the money that ever was in New York, or that ever will be. Give me a holy church, that would live above the world, and the work of salvation would roll on faster than with all the money in Christendom.

Objection. " But we must spend a great deal of money to bring forward an educated ministry."

Ah ! if we had a HOLY ministry, it would be far more important than an educated ministry. If the ministry were holy enough, they would do without so much education. God forbid that I should undervalue an educated ministry. Let ministers be educated as well as they can, the more the better, if they are only holy enough. But it is all a farce to suppose that a literary ministry can convert the world. Let the ministry have the spirit of prayer, let the baptism of the Holy Ghost be upon them, and they will spread the gospel. Only let Christians live as they ought, and the church would shake the world. If Christians in

New York would do it, the report would soon fill every ship that leaves the port, and waft the news on every wind, till the earth was full of excitement and inquiry, and conversions would multiply like the drops of morning dew.

Suppose you were to give up your business, and devote yourselves entirely to the work of extending the gospel. The church once did so, and you know what followed. When that little band in Jerusalem gave up their business and spent their time in the work of God, salvation spread like a wave. And I believe, if the whole Christian church were to turn right out, and convert the world, it would be done in a very short time.

And further, the fact is, that you would not be required to give up your business. If Christians would do business in the spirit of the gospel, they would soon engross the business of the world. Only let the world see, that if they go to a Christian to do business, he will not only deal honestly, but benevolently, that he will actually consult the interest of the person he deals with, as if it were his own interest, and who would deal with anybody else ? What merchant would go to an ungodly man to trade, who he knew would try to get the advantage of him, and cheat him, while he knew that there were Christian merchants to deal with, that would consult his interests as much as they do their own ? Indeed, it is a known fact, that there are now Christian merchants in this city, who regulate the prices of the articles they deal in. Merchants come in from the country, and inquire around to see how they can buy goods, and they go to these men to know exactly what articles are worth at a fair price, and govern themselves accordingly.

The advantage, then, is all on one side. The church can make it for the interest of the ungodly to do business on right principles. The church can regulate the business of the world, and woe to them if they do not.

2. In regard to fashion.

Objection. "Is it best for Christians to be singular?"

Certainly; Christians are bound to be singular. They are called to be a peculiar people, that is, a singular people, essentially different from the rest of mankind. To maintain that we are not to be singular, is the same as to maintain that we are to be conformed to the world. "Be not singular," that is, be like the world. In other words, "Be ye conformed to the world." This is the direct opposite to the command in the text.

But the question now regards fashion, in dress, equipage, and so on. And here I will confess that I was formerly myself in error. I believed, and I taught, that the best way for Christians to pursue, was to dress so as not to be noticed, to follow the fashions and changes so as not to appear singular, and that nobody would be led to think of their being different from others in these particulars. But I have seen my error, and now wonder greatly at my former blindness. It is your duty to dress so plain as to show to the world, that you place no sort of reliance in the things of fashion, and set no value at all on them, but despise and neglect them altogether. But unless you are singular, unless you separate yourselves from the fashions of the world, you show that you do value them. There is no way in which you can bear a proper testimony by your lives against the fashions of the world, but by dressing plain. I do not mean that you should *study singularity*, but that you should consult *convenience and economy*, although it may be singular.

Objection. "But if we dress plain, the attention of people will be taken with it."

The reason of it is this, so few do it that it is a novelty, and everybody stares when they see a professing Christian so strict as to disregard the fashions. Let them all do it, and the only thing you show by it is that you are a Chris tian, and do not wish to be confounded with the ungodly. Would it not tell on the pride of the world, if all the Christians in it were united in bearing a practical testimony against its vain show.

Objection. "But in this way you carry religion too far away from the multitude. It is better not to set up an artificial distinction between the church and the world."

The direct reverse of this is true. The nearer you bring the church to the world, the more you annihilate the reasons that ought to stand out in view of the world, for their changing sides and coming over to the church. Unless you go right out from them, and show that you are not of them in any respect, and carry the church so far as to have a broad interval between saints and sinners, how can you make the ungodly feel that so great a change is necessary.

Objection. "But this change which is necessary is a change of heart."

True; but will not a change of heart produce a change of life?

Objection. "You will throw obstacles in the way of persons becoming Christians. Many respectable people will become disgusted with religion, and if they cannot be allowed to dress and be Christians, they will take to the world altogether."

This is just about as reasonable as it would be for a temperance man to think he must get drunk now and then, to avoid disgusting the intemperate, and to retain his influence over them. The truth is, that persons ought to know, and ought to see in the lives of professing Christians, that if they embrace religion, they must be weaned from the world, and must give up the love of the world, and its pride, and show, and folly, and live a holy life, in watchfulness, and self-denial, and active benevolence,

Objection. "Is it not better for us to disregard this altogether, and not pay any attention to such little things, and let them take their course; let the milliner and mantua-maker do as they please, and follow the usages of society in which we live, and the circle in which we move?"

Is this the way to show contempt for the fashions of the world? Do people ordinarily take this course of showing contempt for a thing, to practice it? Why, the way to show your abhorrence of the world is to follow along in the customs and the fashions of the world! Precious reasoning this.

Objection. "No matter how we dress, if our hearts are right?"

Your heart right! Then your heart may be right when your conduct is all wrong. Just as well might the profane swearer say, "No matter what words I speak, if my heart is right." No, your heart is not right, unless your conduct is right. What is outward conduct, but the acting out of the heart? If your heart was right, you would not wish to follow the fashions of the world.

Objection. "What is the standard of dress? I do not see the use of all your preaching, and laying down rules about plain dress, unless you give us a standard."

This is a mighty stumbling block with many. But to my mind the matter is extremely simple. The whole can be comprised in two simple rules. One is—Be sure, in all your equipage, and dress, and furniture, to show that you have no fellowship with the designs and principles of those who are aiming to set off themselves, and to gain the applause of men. The other is—Let economy be first consulted, and then convenience. Follow christian economy; that is, save all you can for Christ's service; and then, let things be as convenient as Christian economy will admit.

Objection. "Would you have us all to turn Quakers, and put on their plain dress?"

Who does not know, that the plain dress of the Quakers has won for them the respect of all the thinking part of the ungodly in the community? Now, if they had coupled with this, the zeal for God, and the weanedness from the world, and the contempt for rishes, and the self-denying labor for the conversion of sinners to Christ, which the gospel enjoins, and the clear views of the plan of salvation which the gospel inculcates, they would long since have converted the world. And if all Christians would imitate them in their plain dress, (I do not mean the precise cut and fashion of their dress, but in a *plain* dress, throwing contempt upon the fashions of the world,) who can doubt that the conversion of the world would hasten on apace?

Objection. "Would you make us all into Methodists?"

Who does not know that the Methodists, when they were noted for their plain dress, and for renouncing the fashions and show of the world, used to have power with God in prayer—and that they had the universal respect of the world as sincere Christians. And who does not know that since they have laid aside this peculiarity, and conformed to the world in dress and other things, and seemed to be trying to lift themselves up as a denomination, and gain influence with the world, they are losing the power of prayer? Would to God they had never thrown down this wall. It was one of the leading excellences of Wesley's system, to have his followers distinguished from others by a plain dress.

Objection. "We may be proud of a plain dress as well as of a fashionable dress. The Quakers are as proud as we are."

So may any good thing be abused. But that is no reason why it should not be used, if it can be shown to be good. I put it back to the objector—Is that any reason why a Christian female, who fears God and loves the souls of men, should neglect the means which may make an impression that she is separated from the world, and pour contempt on the fashions of the ungodly, in which they are dancing their way to hell?

Objection. "This is a small thing, and ought not to take up so much of a minister's time in the pulpit."

This is an objection often heard from worldly professors. But the minister that fears God will not be deterred by it. He will pursue the subject, until such professing Christians are cut off from their conformity to the world, or cut off from the church. It is not merely the dress, as dress but it is the conformity to the world in dress and fashion, that is the great stumbling-block in the way of sinners. How can the world be converted, while professing Christians are conformed to the world? What good will it do to give money to send the gospel to the heathen, when Christians live so at home? Well might the heathen ask, "What profit will it be to become Christians, when those who are Christians are pursuing the world with all the hot haste of the ungodly?" The great thing necessary for the church is to break off from conformity to the world, and then they will have power with God in prayer, and the Holy Ghost will descend and bless their efforts, and the world will be converted.

Objection. "But if we dress so, we shall be called fanatics."

Whatever the ungodly may call you, fanatics, Methodists, or anything, you will be known as Christians, and in the secret consciences of men will be acknowledged as such. It is not in the power of unbelievers to pour contempt on a holy church, that are separated from the world. How was it with the early Christians? They lived separate from the world, and it made such an impression, that even infidel writers say of them, "These men win the hearts of the mass of the people, because they give themselves up to deeds of charity, and pour contempt on the world." Depend upon it, if Christians would live so now, the last effort of hell would soon be expended in vain to defeat the spread of the gospel. Wave after wave would flow abroad, till the highest mountain tops were covered with the waters of life.

3. In regard to politics.

Objection. "In this way, by acting on these principles, and refusing to unite with the world in politics, we could have no influence in government and national affairs."

I answer, first, It is so now. Christians, as such, have no influence. There is not a Christian principle adopted because it is Christian, or because it is according to the law of God.

I answer, secondly, If there is no other way for Christians to have an influence in the government, but by becoming conformed to the world in their habitual principles and parties, then let the ungodly take the government and manage it in their own way, and do you go and serve God.

I answer, thirdly, No such result will follow. Directly the reverse of this would be the fact. Only let it be known that Christian citizens will on no account assist bad men into office; only let it be known that the church will go only for men that will aim at the public good, and both parties will be sure to set up such men. And in this way, the church could legitimately exert an influence, by compelling all parties to bring forward only men who are worthy of an honest man's support.

Objection. "In this way the church and the world will be arrayed against each other."

The world is too selfish for this. You cannot make parties so. Such a line can never be a permanent division. For one year the ungodly might unite against the church, and leave Christians in a small minority. But in the end, the others would form two parties, each courting the suffrages of Christians, by offering candidates such as Christians can conscientiously vote for.

CONCLUSION

1. By non-conformity to the world, you may save much money for doing good.

In one year a greater fund might be saved by the church than has ever been raised for the spread of the gospel.

2. By non-conformity to the world, a great deal of time may be saved for doing good, that is now consumed and wasted in following the fashions, and obeying the maxims, and joining in the pursuits of the world.

3. At the same time, Christians in this way would preserve their peace of conscience, would enjoy communion with God, would have the spirit of prayer, and would possess far greater usefulness.

Is it not time something was done? Is it not time that some church struck out a path, that should not be conformed to the world, but should be according to the example and Spirit of Christ?

You profess that you want to have sinners converted. But what avails it, if they sink right back again into conformity with the world? Brethren, I confess, I am filled with pain in view of the conduct of the church. Where are the proper results of the glorious revivals we have had? I believe they were genuine revivals of religion and outpourings of the Holy Ghost, that the church has enjoyed the last ten years. I believe the converts of the last ten years are among the best Christians in the land. Yet after all, the great body of them are a disgrace to religion. Of what use would it be to have a thousand members added to the church, to be just such as are now in it? Would religion be any more honored by it, in the estimation of ungodly men? One holy church, that are really crucified to the world, and the world to them, would do more to recommend christianity, than all the churches in the country, living as they now do. O, if I had strength of body to go through the churches again, instead of preaching to convert sinners, I would preach to bring up the churches to the gospel standard of holy living. Of what use is it to convert sinners, and make them such Christians as these? Of what use is it to try to convert sinners, and make them feel there is something in religion, and when they go to trade with you, or meet you in the street, have you contradict it all, and tell them, by your conformity to the world, that there is nothing in it?

Where shall I look, where shall the Lord look, for a church like the first church, that will come out from the world, and be separate, and give themselves up to serve God? O, if this church would do so. But it is of little use to make Christians if they are not better. Do not understand me as saying that the converts made in our revivals are spurious. But they live so as to be a disgrace to religion. They are so stumbled by old professors that many of them do more hurt than good. The more there are of them, the more occasion infidelity seems to find for her jeers and scoffs.

Now, do you believe that God commands you not to be conformed to the world? Do you believe it? And dare you obey it, let people say what they will about you? Dare you now separate yourselves from the world, and never again be controlled by its maxims, and never again copy its practices, and never again will be whiffled here and there by its fashions? I know a man that lives so, I could mention his name, he pays no attention to the customs of the world in this respect, and what is the result? Wherever that man goes, he leaves the impression behind that he is a Christian. O, if one church would do so, and would engage in it with all the energy that men of the world engage in their business, they would turn the world upside down.

Will you do so? Will you break off from the world now, and enter into covenant with God, and declare that you will dare to be singular enough to be separate from the world, and from this time set your faces as a flint to obey God, let the world say what they will? Dare you do it? Will you do it?

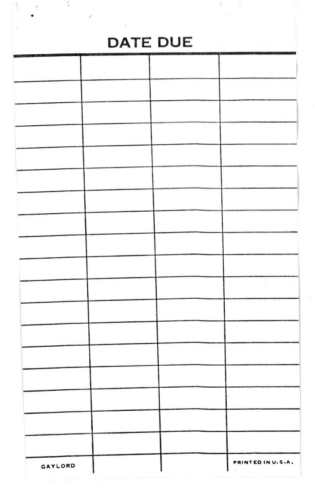

DATE DUE

GAYLORD

PRINTED IN U.S.A.